The Burrell Collection

ART, ARCHITECTURE AND REGENERATION

Text by Robert Gartshore

Photography by Iona Shepherd

Scala Arts & Heritage Publishers

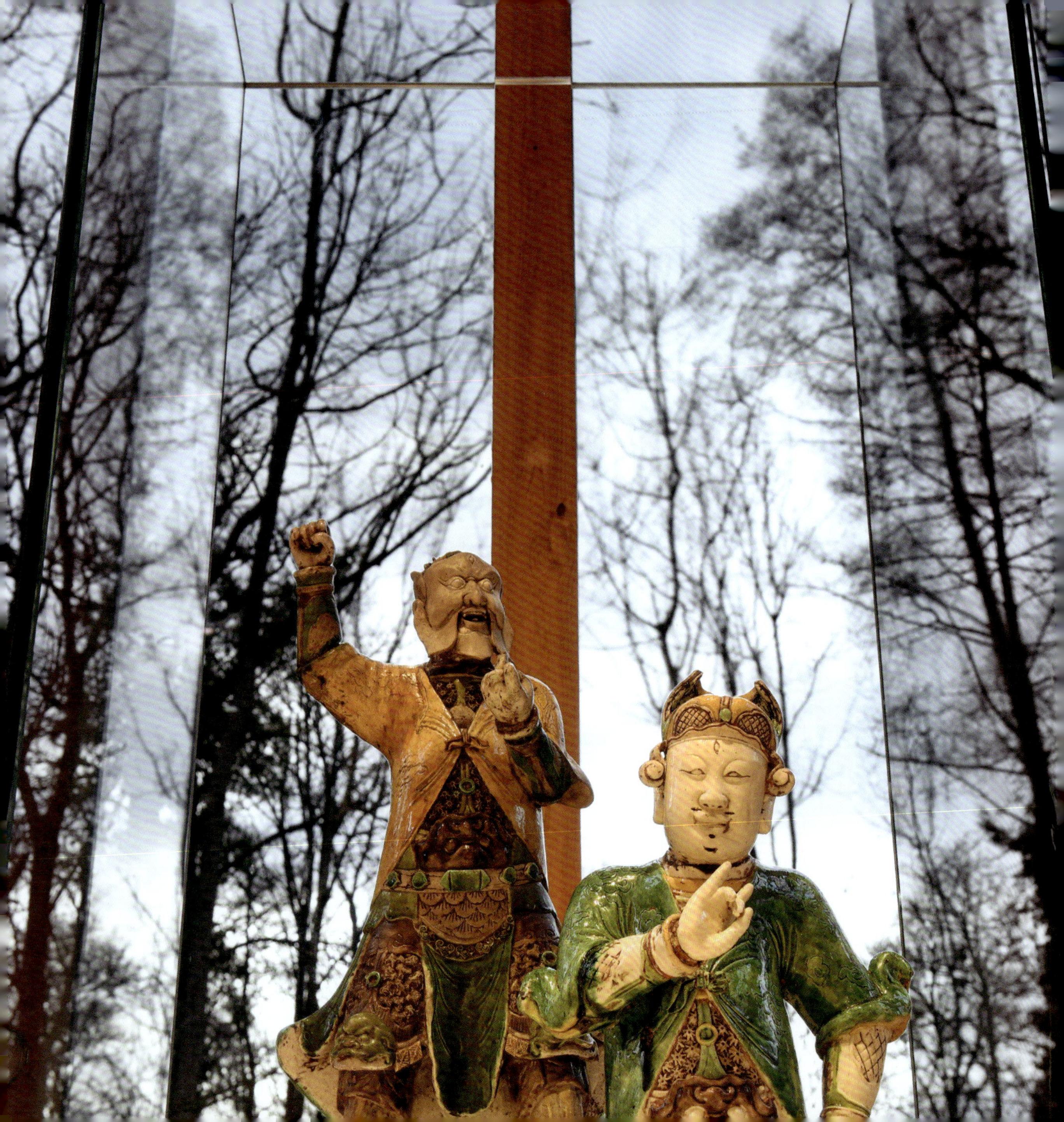

CONTENTS

INTRODUCTION

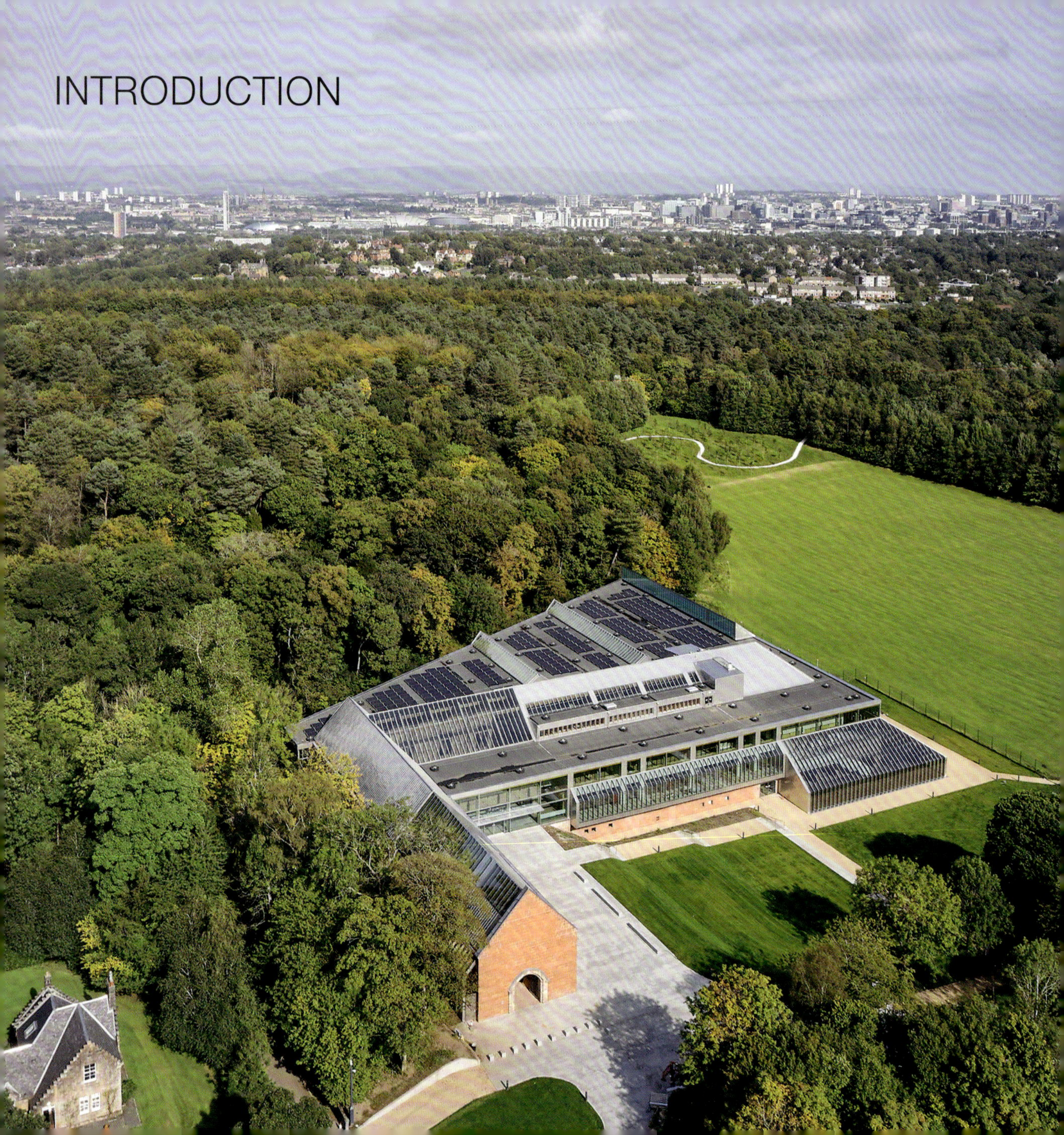

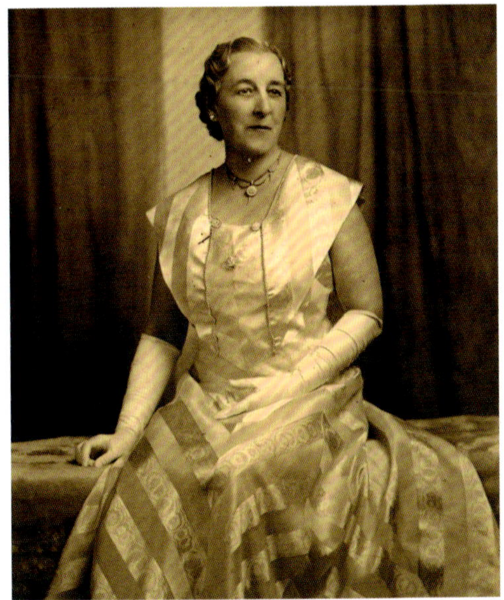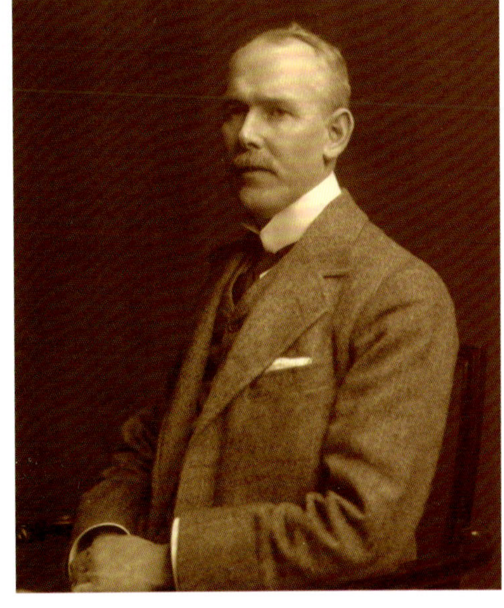

Most Glaswegians are fond of a good tale, and that of the city's Burrell Collection is an absorbing one, with a cast of characters and a narrative that tells the story of human creativity and art spanning more than six millennia. It is a unique combination of museum collection and building, both of national and international significance, situated within a historical country park that is home to an ancient woodland and an Iron Age fort that is as old as some of the collection objects.

The protagonists of the story are Sir William and Constance, Lady Burrell, both successful investors in the shipping trade who spent much of their wealth and life amassing a vast and eclectic collection of astonishing art objects from around the world.

Born in Glasgow, William Burrell (1861–1958) became one of the world's greatest art collectors. He began collecting items of interest to him in his early teens, continuing to do so throughout his lifetime. In 1944, he and his wife Constance (1875–1961) gave their collection of more than 6,000 art objects to the City of Glasgow, a bestowal described at the time as 'one of the greatest gifts ever made to any city in the world'.[1]

Often described as a 'canny collector', William Burrell's manner of collecting was somewhat different to those of his contemporaries and far wealthier Americans. He was very specific about the art objects he wanted, and was prepared to negotiate hard to get them at a price he considered acceptable: 'He approached his art purchases as

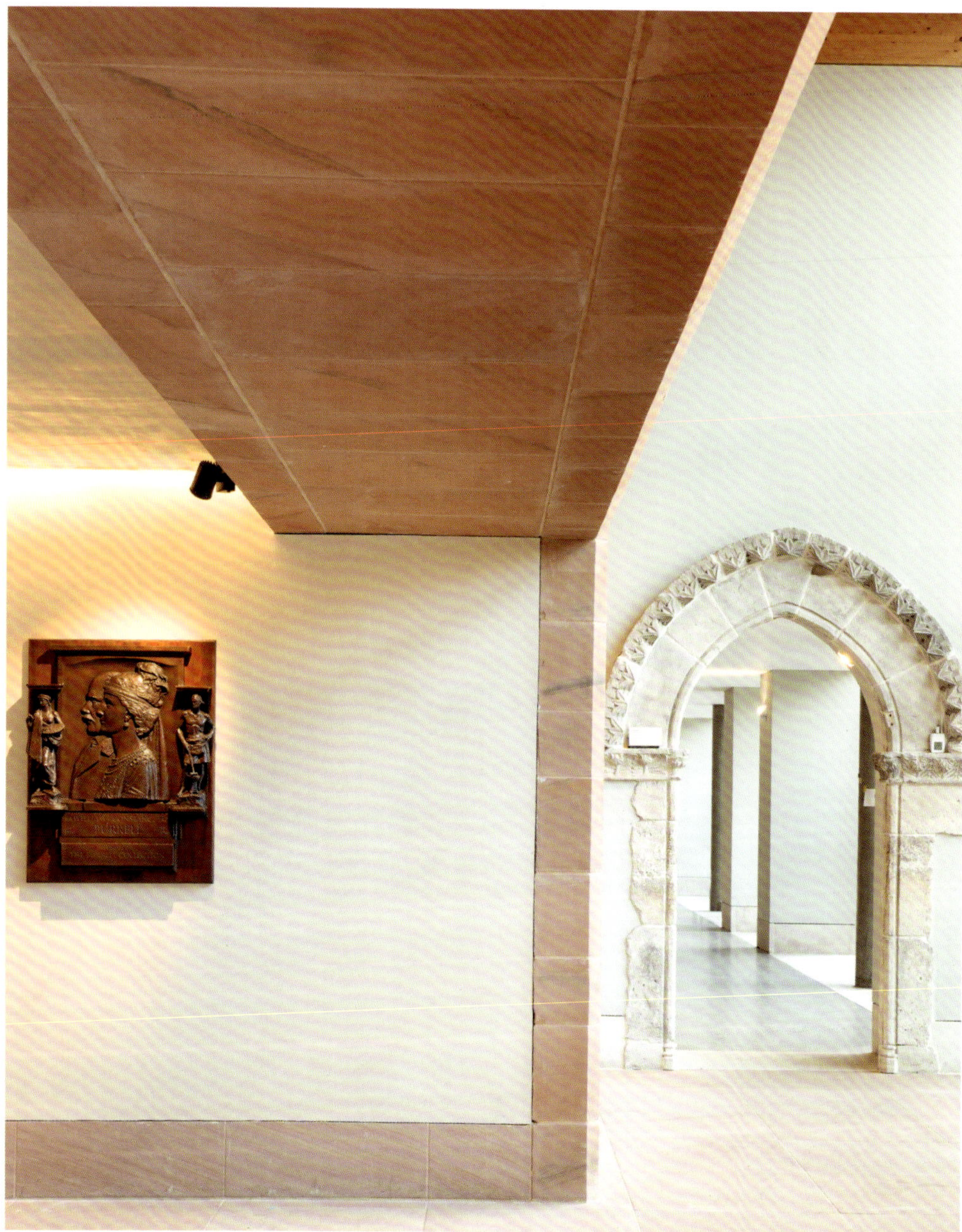

The additional entrance interior, introduced in 2022, with Alexander Stoddart's relief sculpture of Sir William and Constance, Lady Burrell on the left.

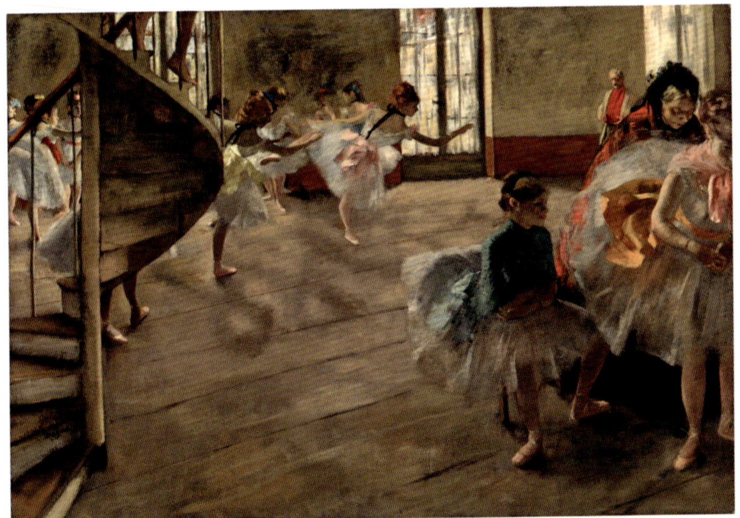

Edgar Degas's *The Rehearsal*, c. 1874, bought by William Burrell in 1926 and described by him as the best picture the artist ever painted.

business transactions; although he let his heart select the objects, it was his head that bought them.'[2]

Constance Burrell was a wealthy businesswoman, and also a major investor in Sir William's shipping company. A philanthropist, she was actively involved in charitable work relating to social health and medical matters. She shared her husband's great passion for art collecting, and by the time of his death they had added another 3,000 objects to their gift to the city. However, the Burrells' legacy is not merely the physical objects they collected; it is also the stories the pieces tell – from the places they were made to the makers who created them.

In a series of notebooks, William Burrell kept careful records of what he bought and what he paid.

FINDING A HOME FOR THE COLLECTION

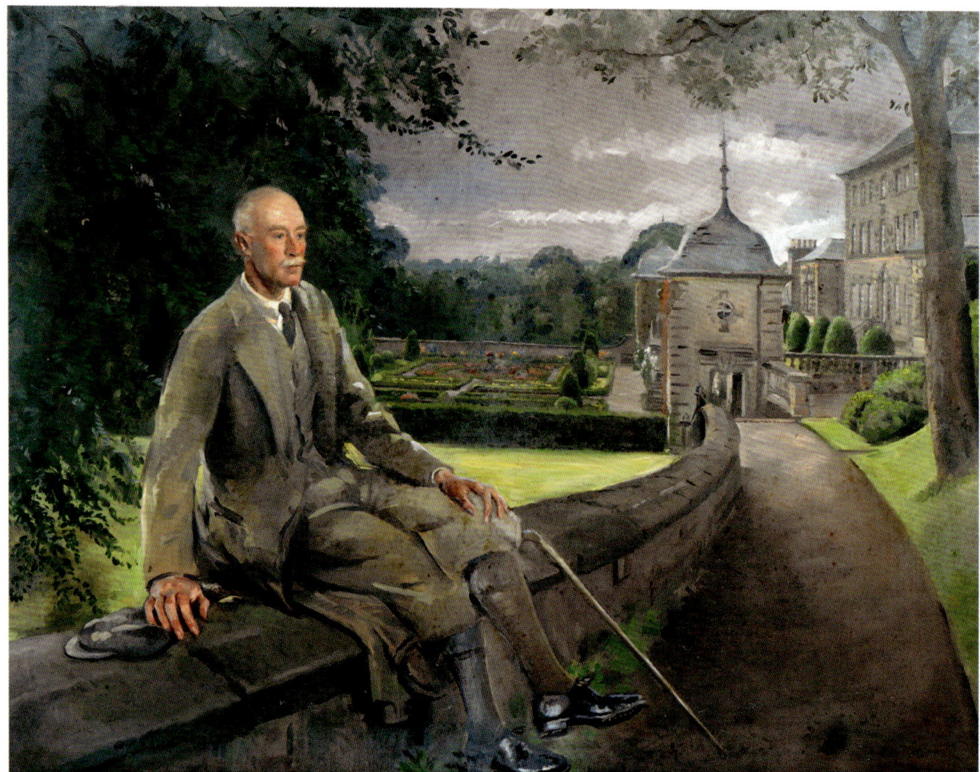

Sir John Stirling Maxwell, with Pollok House in the background. Painting by William Ranken, 1922, oil on canvas.

The Burrells' exacting conditions in gifting their collection to the city included specific requirements for the location of a new building to house it. They stipulated that the collection be housed within 4 miles (6 km) of Killearn, Stirlingshire, not less than 16 miles (26 km) from Glasgow city centre, and within a natural setting. This would reflect the setting of the Burrells' own rural house at Hutton Castle in Berwickshire, where William and Constance lived among the collection, but would also prevent environmental contamination of the works from industrial and domestic air pollutants from chimneys burning fossil fuels.

Glasgow City Council not unreasonably expressed concerns that it would be difficult to administer such a significant museum collection so far from Glasgow, and that the location would also restrict the number of visitors. After much persuasion, Sir William relented and the Dougalston Estate in Milngavie, on the outskirts of Glasgow, was considered. This was eventually rejected by Burrell due to the planned development of the site for coal mining, and the search for a suitable home continued. Burrell did not manage to find a home for the collection before he died, and ultimately the final decision was left to the Burrell Trustees.

However, wider political matters in the UK would soon help find a solution to this seemingly impossible condition. In 1956 the Clean Air Act was passed by the UK government, requiring the country's industrial cities to tackle the problem of air pollution, and in 1959 Glasgow began a smoke-control campaign which was to make it one of the cleanest industrial cities in Britain. The Act paved the way for an investigation into the viability of Sir John Stirling Maxwell's Pollok Estate, much closer to the city centre, as a suitable site for the collection.

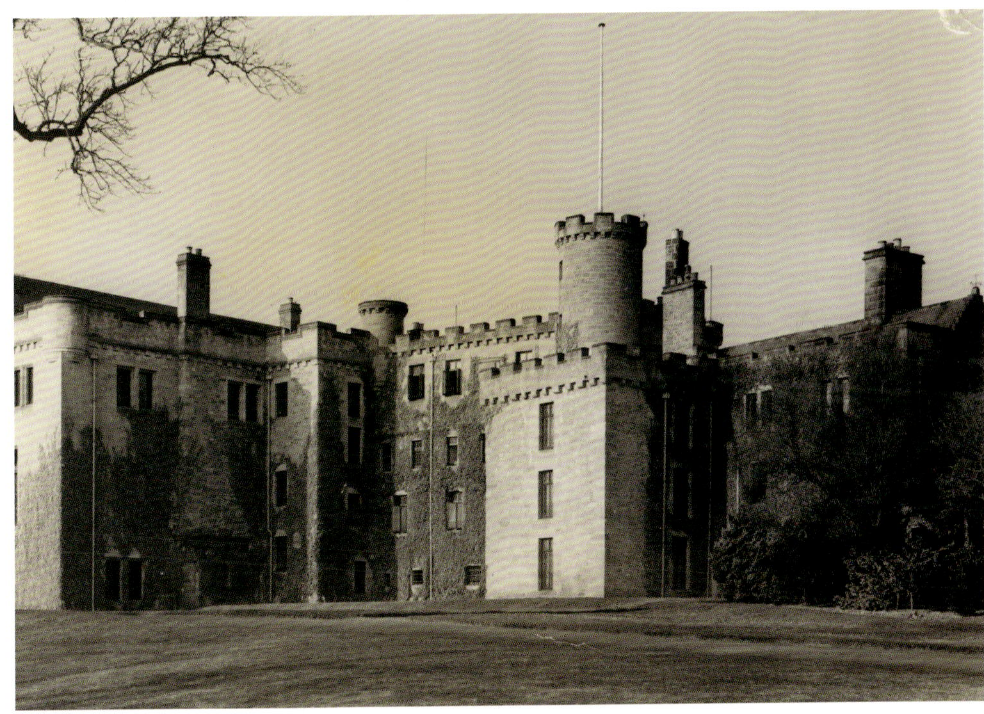

Hutton Castle, the Burrells' home in the Scottish Borders near Berwick-upon-Tweed.

Wealth at a cost

The land on which the Burrell Collection stands is part of the Nether Pollok Estate (now Pollok Country Park) that had been owned by the Maxwell family for over 750 years. From the 1750s the wealth of the estate was closely tied to profits generated from transatlantic slavery.

Sir Walter Maxwell, 4th Baronet of Pollok, was a major financier of the Glasgow West Indies trade. In 1761 he established the Thistle Bank in partnership with Glasgow's leading plantation owners. His younger brother James Maxwell managed a plantation on the Caribbean island of St Kitts in the 1750s where he met Frances (Fanny) Colhoun, daughter of a leading plantation owner. When Walter Maxwell and his infant son died in 1762, the estate was inherited by James, who became 6th Baronet of Pollok. He returned to Glasgow and married Fanny whose dowry and later inheritance added considerably to the family fortune. As well as inheriting the Pollok Estate, James Maxwell also took over his brother's business interests in the Thistle Bank. He used his wealth to upgrade Pollok House, the Georgian mansion built by his father in 1752, and significantly developed the estate.

In 1815 the Maxwell family combined with the Stirling family when James and Fanny's granddaughter Elizabeth married Archibald Stirling of Keir. Archibald Stirling was a major plantation owner in Jamaica and received significant compensation (about £20 million in today's terms) for the loss of 690 enslaved Africans under the government abolition scheme of 1834. When the Maxwell male heirs died out in 1865, Archibald and Elizabeth's son William inherited the Pollok Estate, and the family then became known as the Stirling Maxwells. William's son, Sir John Stirling Maxwell (1866–1956), became the 10th Baronet of Pollok in 1878 and set about improving the estate, enlarging Pollok House and expanding the art collection that he had inherited from his father.

Sir John Stirling Maxwell was a friend and art collector rival of Sir William Burrell. They shared many interests and sat on several committees together, including the National Trust for Scotland, the National Galleries of Scotland, and Provand's Lordship, a medieval residence built around 1471 and now a house museum displaying a collection of furniture, some of it donated by the Burrells. They were also members of the Glasgow Conservative Association and Society of Antiquaries of Scotland. In 1901, they collaborated on the Glasgow International Exhibition, and their complementary art collections were occasionally lent to the same exhibitions.

However, Burrell's connection to the Stirling Maxwells stretched back to 1883 when the Burrell family shipping line had joined forces with John Stirling, a cousin of Archibald Stirling of Keir, who had acquired the family's West Indies shipping interests in 1866. In 1883, Burrell and Stirling established a new shipping business known as the Clyde

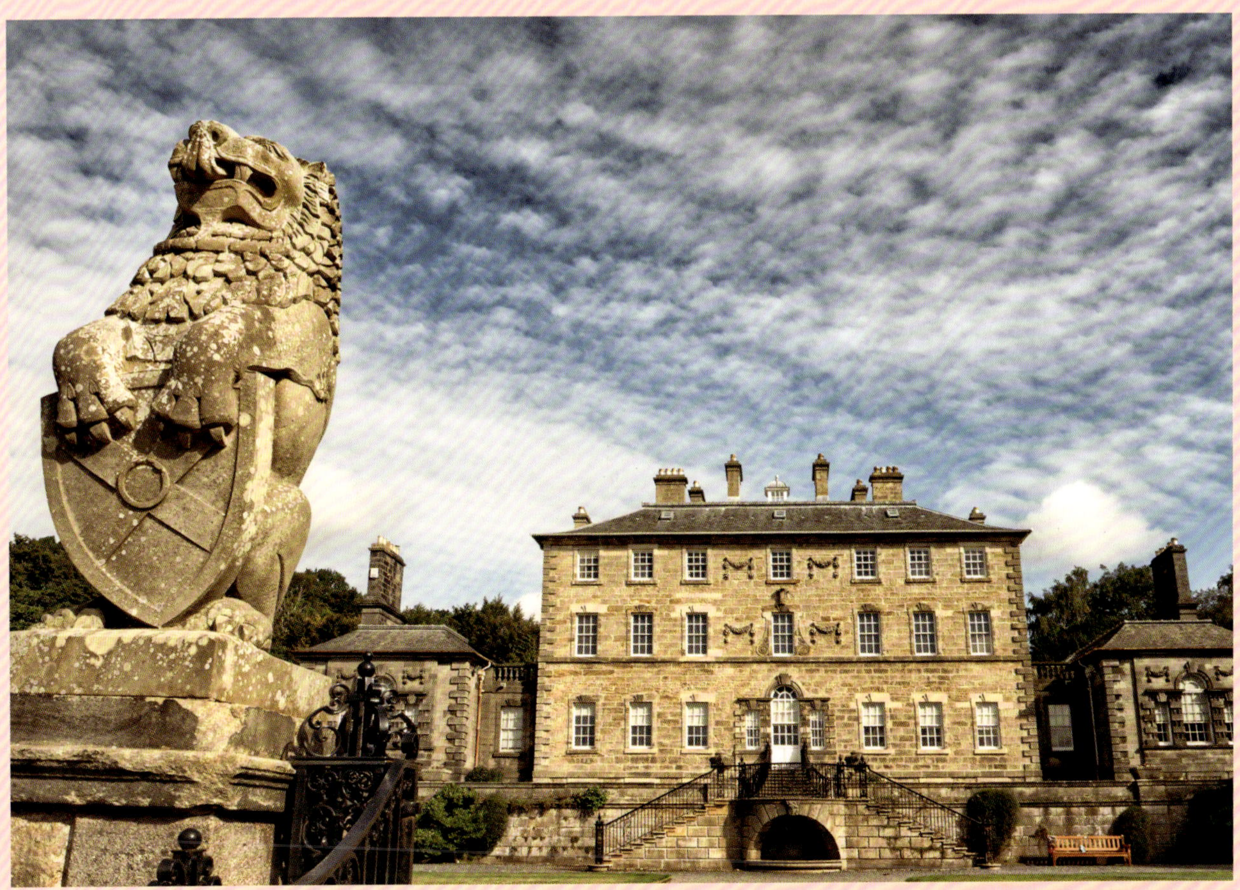

Pollok House, the home of Sir John Stirling Maxwell, in Pollok Country Park.

Line, which ran a regular steamship service between Glasgow and Jamaica. This helped establish William Burrell as one of the leading shipowners in Glasgow and enabled him to further exploit the people and products of empire for his own profit. It was these profits that financed his art collection.

Both the Pollok Estate and Burrell's trading links are deeply connected with the British Empire and the exploitation of enslaved and indentured labour in the Caribbean. It is important to recognise that the fortunes and collections of both these families, and the land on which the museum sits, are closely linked to a history of injustice and suffering.

Text by Dr Martin Bellamy

A gift to the city

Stirling Maxwell appreciated the natural environment and the benefits of parkland spaces within the city, and wanted to ensure citizens could enjoy these. In 1887 he had gifted land from his estate to the burgh of Pollokshields for the development of a burgh hall and public gardens. (The park is now known as Maxwell Park and contains many plants and flowers that were taken from the gardens of his home, Pollok House.) He had long invited the public into his Pollok Estate, and sporting, church and school groups were regular visitors. For many years he opened the grounds to the public at weekends during the summer, and in 1911 this was extended to every day of the week. He also provided land to the public for garden allotments. In 1939 he secured the first Conservation Agreement with the National Trust for Scotland to preserve the estate's natural and built heritage.

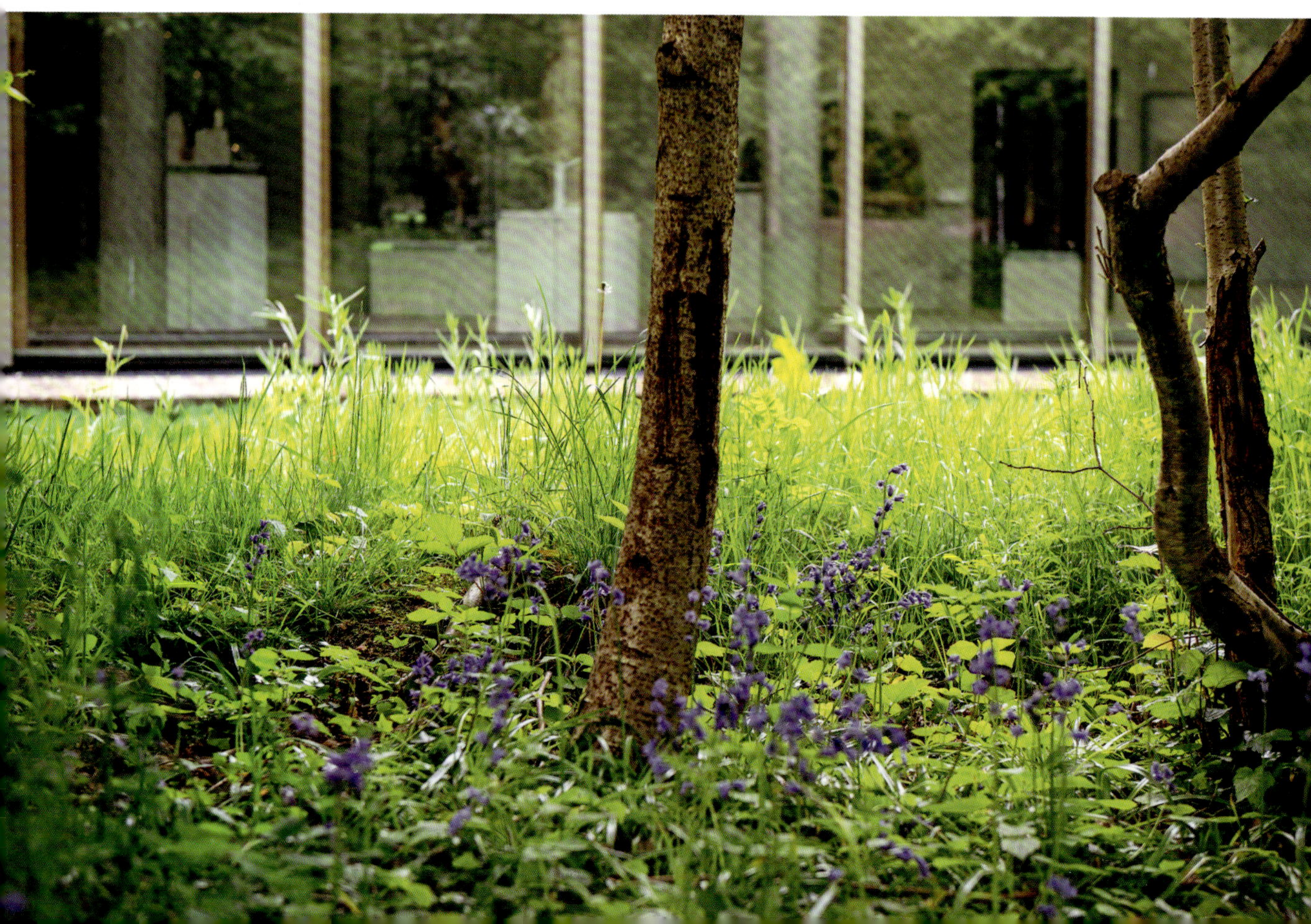

Each year, the Burrell Collection is surrounded by woodland bluebells.

Following Stirling Maxwell's death in 1956, his daughter Anne Maxwell Macdonald (1906–2011) inherited the family's estate and ancestral home. She was keen to secure an appropriate future for the estate, and in 1962 initiated discussions with the National Trust for Scotland about gifting it to the Trust. On hearing this, the Lord Provost of Glasgow, Peter Meldrum, suggested it might be a suitable location for the Burrells' collection.

In December 1963 Anne, along with representatives from the National Trust for Scotland and the Burrell Trustees, gathered in the park to assess the suitability of the site, and with some surprise and relief all were in favour of the location. However, the financial commitment was too great for the National Trust, and despite protracted discussions with the Glasgow Corporation, no final agreement could be reached. In 1966, Richard Buchanan, a Glasgow Member of Parliament and former city councillor, brought a debate to the House of Commons to move matters forward. An excerpt of his speech from Parliament records is captured below:

I implore my ex-colleagues of Glasgow Corporation to take their courage in both hands. Glasgow has always played her part in stimulating and encouraging the arts. In this respect a responsibility has been placed on them, and I ask them to stop this delicate, dithering, dickering diplomacy. Delay simply plays into the hands of the Philistines in their midst. If the opportunity is lost here, it may never recur. I ask my former colleagues of Glasgow Corporation to 'go it alone' if need be. They can do this sort of thing better than most.[3]

Buchanan's actions had the desired effect, with the Under-Secretary of State for Scotland, Bruce Millan, offering £250,000 in government support. When added to William Burrell's financial gift of £750,000 this provided the Corporation with a quarter of the amount estimated to erect a new building. An agreement was eventually reached in 1967, and Anne Maxwell Macdonald consented to gift the 360-acre Pollok Estate, with its formally designed landscapes, charming walled gardens, and natural woodland walks and habitat, to the City of Glasgow. A home for the collection had finally been found.

The estate is Glasgow's largest green space and is only about 3 miles (4.8 km) from the city centre, providing the perfect natural setting and home for the Burrells' collection. The shared interests, histories and legacies of two philanthropic Glasgow families were thus brought together, setting the stage for the commissioning of the building visitors now enjoy.

Glasgow – The 'Dear Green Place'

It is worth pausing at this point to note the wider sociocultural landscape of Glasgow at the time and the significance of the location of the Burrell Collection within Pollok Country Park. The city has a long tradition of siting museums and libraries in public parks with the aim of combining both physical and mental well-being for its citizens. This dates back to an 1869 essay titled 'Museums for the People'[4] by the English naturalist, evolutionist, geographer, anthropologist, and social critic and theorist Alfred Russel Wallace.

A few weeks after Wallace's essay was published, Glasgow Parks and Galleries Trust was formed, giving further impetus to Glasgow's wider social-reform aspirations and laying out the plans for housing the city's first municipal museum, the City Industrial Museum (1870) – now Kelvingrove Art Gallery and Museum – in Kelvingrove Mansion within Kelvingrove Park, and the construction of the People's Palace and Winter Gardens (1898) on Glasgow Green.

Locating the Burrells' collection within Pollok Country Park reinforced the importance of the well-being of the citizens of Glasgow, and represents their proud history of creating and protecting civic parks and greens. Glasgow is literally a 'green valley/glen' – the translation of its Gaelic name, Glaschu. Etymology traces the origins back to the Brythonic Celtic but it is now more commonly and affectionately known as 'the dear green place'. There are more than 3,500 hectares of green space in the city, and more of this is accessible than in any other Scottish city. Parks and open areas are recognised as providing a vital and vibrant contribution to the daily lives of the people who live in, work in and visit the city.

The significance of Anne Maxwell Macdonald's gifting of the Pollok Estate to the city should therefore not be underestimated. As a working country park and a natural public wilderness, it offered a different experience to the city's other municipal parks. It not only enabled William Burrell's original and exacting requirements for the housing of the collection to be realised, but also provided a rare architectural design opportunity to explore the relationship between art and nature, and to exploit how this natural setting could enhance the experience for museum visitors.

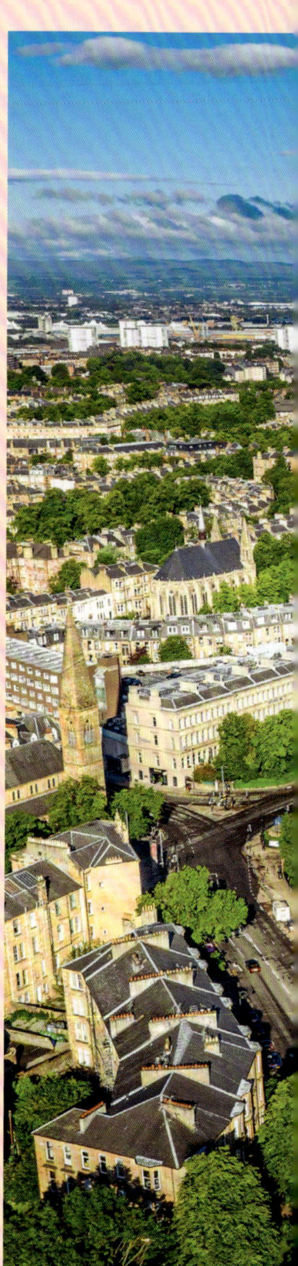

View of the West End of Glasgow, looking west, showing the extent of green space in the city. The glass house buildings are the Kibble Palace and the Botanic Gardens. Photographer HawkAye.

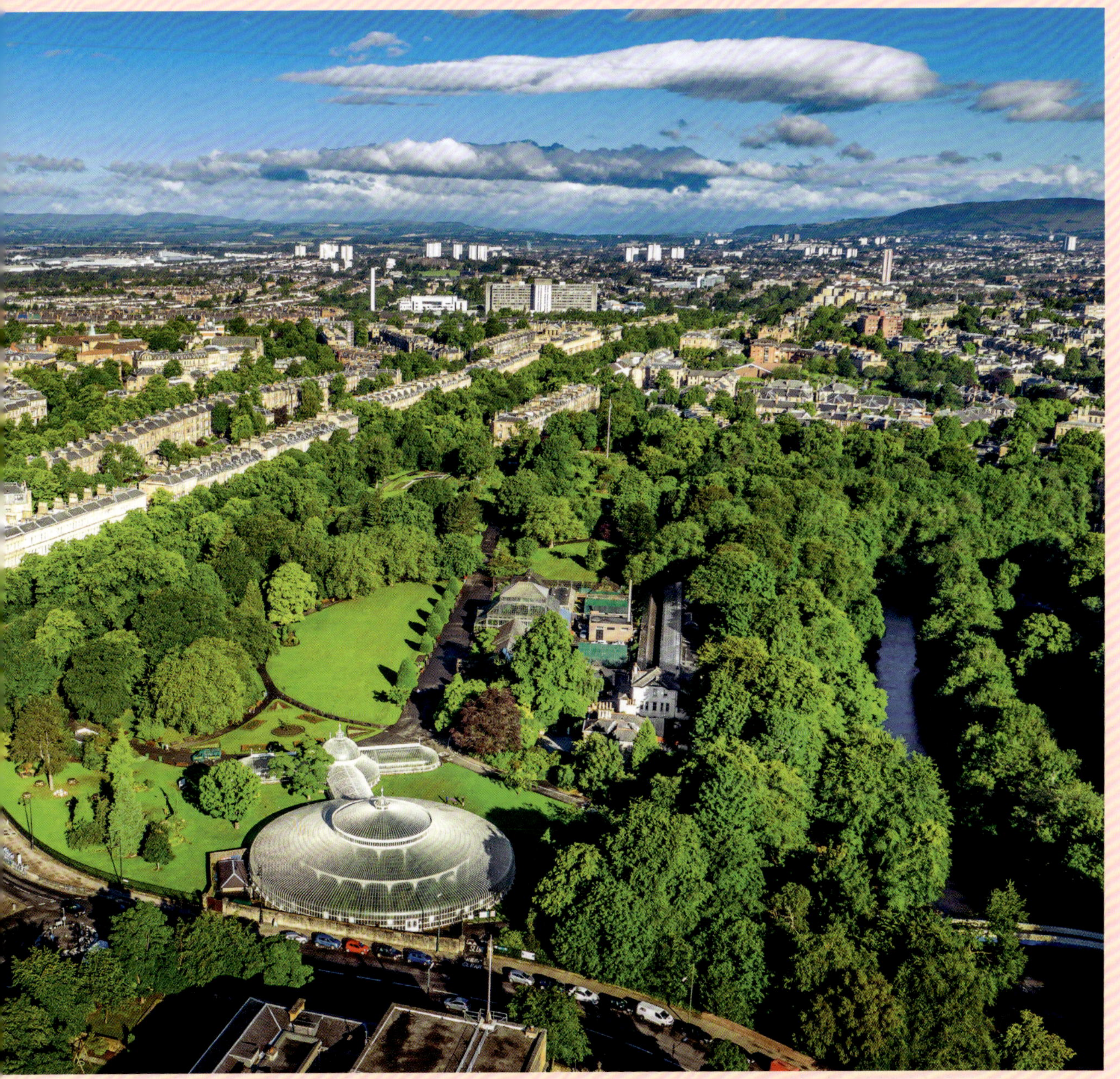

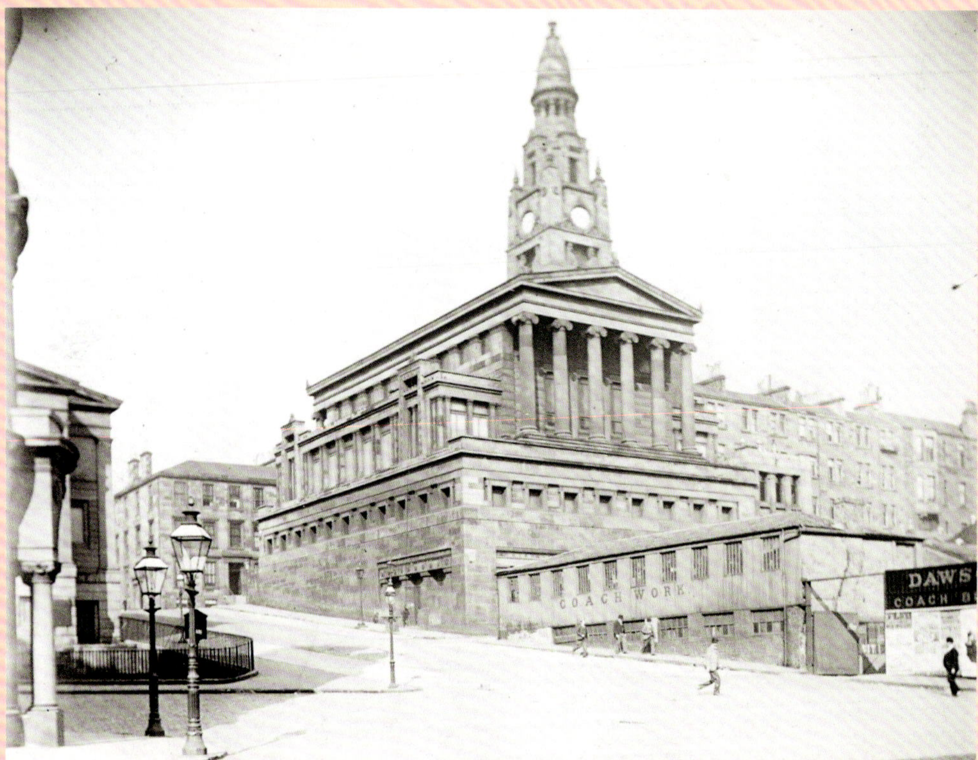

Black-and-white photographic negative depicting Alexander 'Greek' Thomson's St Vincent Free Church, Glasgow, about 1895.

The 'Glasgow Style'

Glasgow has traditionally been a place of enterprise and innovation, embracing international ideas and adapting them to form a particular vision for the city. This is evident in its architecture of the nineteenth and twentieth centuries, and particularly so in the interpretations of Greek, Egyptian and Levantine architecture by Alexander 'Greek' Thomson (1817–1875), and in the influence of Japanese craft and engineering designs combined with Art Nouveau in the pioneering work of Charles Rennie Mackintosh (1868–1928). In the early 1890s, Mackintosh, along with the artist and designer James Herbert McNair (1868–1955) and the MacDonald sisters, Margaret (1864–1933) and Frances (1873–1921), formed a collaborative group of artists and designers all interested in avant-garde ideas. Their works, along with those of a wider group of Glaswegian artists, became known as the 'Glasgow Style'. Highly influential in the European Art Nouveau movement, the group retains notable international interest to this day.

Embracing modernity

During the nineteenth century, Glasgow enjoyed considerable wealth due to increased global trading opportunities brought about by the Industrial Revolution and the exporting of the ideas of the Scottish Enlightenment in the fields of philosophy, politics, economics, art, science and engineering. Driven by capitalism and innovation, the city became one of the richest and most populated in the world. As a significant global trading port, it attracted cheap migrant labour from the Highlands of Scotland and Ireland, as well as wider migration from Italy and eastern Europe, leading to a rich cultural revolution – a legacy that remains. However, the city could not cope with the rapid rate of population growth, which resulted in the emergence of many slums and a housing and health crisis.

As a councillor (1899–1906), William Burrell became politically active in finding a solution to clearing the slums and improving housing and health. In 1904 he was Convenor of the Police Department's Health sub-committee on 'Uninhabitable Houses, Areas and Back Lands, and Underground Dwellings'.

Whilst there was significant political momentum at this time to resolve the housing crisis, two world wars significantly disrupted actual progress, and it was not until March 1945 that the Glasgow Corporation published a full report that proposed a 50-year plan for the complete regeneration of the city, commonly known as the Bruce Report.[5] This was a utopian vision for the city that embraced the ideas of the Swiss-French architect Le Corbusier (1887–1965). The aim was not just to transform it but to build a new Glasgow as a modern, 'healthy and beautiful city'.

Following further political – and presumably technical – debate surrounding the Bruce Report, the more ambitious city demolition and development proposals were abandoned but the ethos of the proposed plan was generally adopted. This included the demolition of the city centre on a large scale combined with the development of new towns on its outskirts, such as Cumbernauld – at the time one of the best examples of a modernist new town in the UK. Work on the massive redevelopment began in the 1950s, and was finally completed in 1978. It included the construction of the M8 motorway ring road in 1965.

Much has been written about the legacy failures of this regeneration model but there is no doubt that this large-scale utopian vision for Glasgow was bold and demonstrates the city's aspirations and character.

DESIGNING A HOME FOR THE COLLECTION

Burrell had sought his own architectural designs to house the collection. Frank Surgey (1893–1974), a London-based antique dealer and designer who had worked previously for Burrell on the interiors of Hutton Castle, spent over two years in the late 1940s preparing sketch plans for a museum:

I told him I should like the Museum to have the contents shown to look as little like the usual Museum as possible, e.g., to have the contents of the bedroom beds etc. shown in bedrooms instead of all the beds being clubbed together and to have the stained glass shown so that the windows with their vistas would show it to the best advantage instead of all the stained glass being shown as in the Victoria & Albert in the Glass Department – all huddled together.[6]

The proposal was an H-shaped layout in neoclassical style, which Burrell felt 'would be a wonderful building and most suitable'.[7] Surgey's designs were initially developed for a site at Old Ballikinrain House, near Balfron, Stirling. However, the Glasgow Corporation was unable to secure the site, nor one on the Mugdock Castle Estate, near Milngavie, to the north of Glasgow, so it was back to the drawing board.

Burrell next commissioned Murray Adams-Acton (1886–1971), Surgey's business partner, to draw up a set of plans for the potential site on the Dougalston Estate. Adams-Acton's preliminary sketches included neoclassical elements, and an inner courtyard and galleries off a central space. He proposed two floors, and detailed the placement of individual objects in sketch plans illustrating how the architectural collection could be 'assembled harmoniously' within the building. Large parts of the collection were moved into storage at Dougalston House. However, in 1955, with the news that the National Coal Board was investigating the possibility of sinking a mineshaft close to the site, all plans for Dougalston were immediately abandoned.

After Burrell's death it would be the Glasgow City Corporation and the Burrell Trustees who finally managed to find a suitable site and a museum design to house the collection.

Frank Surgey's architectural plan for how the museum to house the Burrells' collection might look.

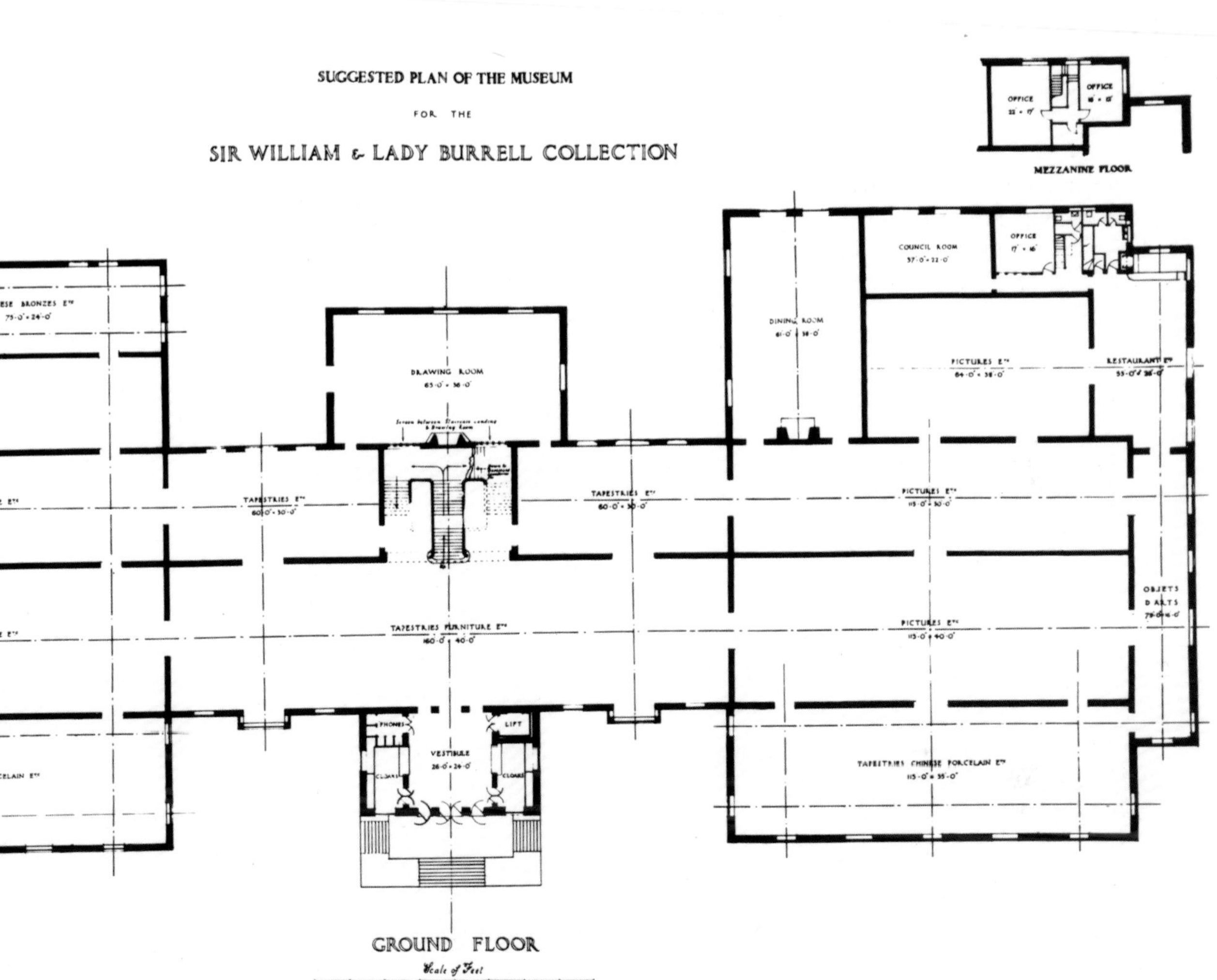

SUGGESTED PLAN OF THE MUSEUM
FOR THE
SIR WILLIAM & LADY BURRELL COLLECTION
MEZZANINE FLOOR
OFFICE
OFFICE
COUNCIL ROOM
OFFICE
CHINESE BRONZES ETC
DRAWING ROOM
DINING ROOM
PICTURES ETC
RESTAURANT ETC
TAPESTRIES ETC
TAPESTRIES ETC
PICTURES ETC
OBJETS D ARTS
TAPESTRIES FURNITURE ETC
PICTURES ETC
PHONES
LIFT
CLOAKS
VESTIBULE
CLOAKS
TAPESTRIES CHINESE PORCELAIN ETC
PORCELAIN ETC
GROUND FLOOR
Scale of Feet

An international architecture competition

Three years after finally securing the Pollok Estate site as a home for the collection, in 1970 the Glasgow City Corporation launched a two-stage international competition to find a suitable architect to meet the requirements of Burrell's deed of gift for the building and display. The competition brief has been widely acclaimed as excellent,[8] and is well recorded in Barnabas Calder's article 'Castles, Cows and Glasshouses: the Burrell Collection Architectural Competition'.[9] It was very prescriptive in terms of entry submissions and specifications, stipulating that the collection needed to be the most important aspect of the design:

The donors have recommended that the Collection, so far as possible, be shown as it would be if in a private house, with as little resemblance to a formal museum as possible.[10]

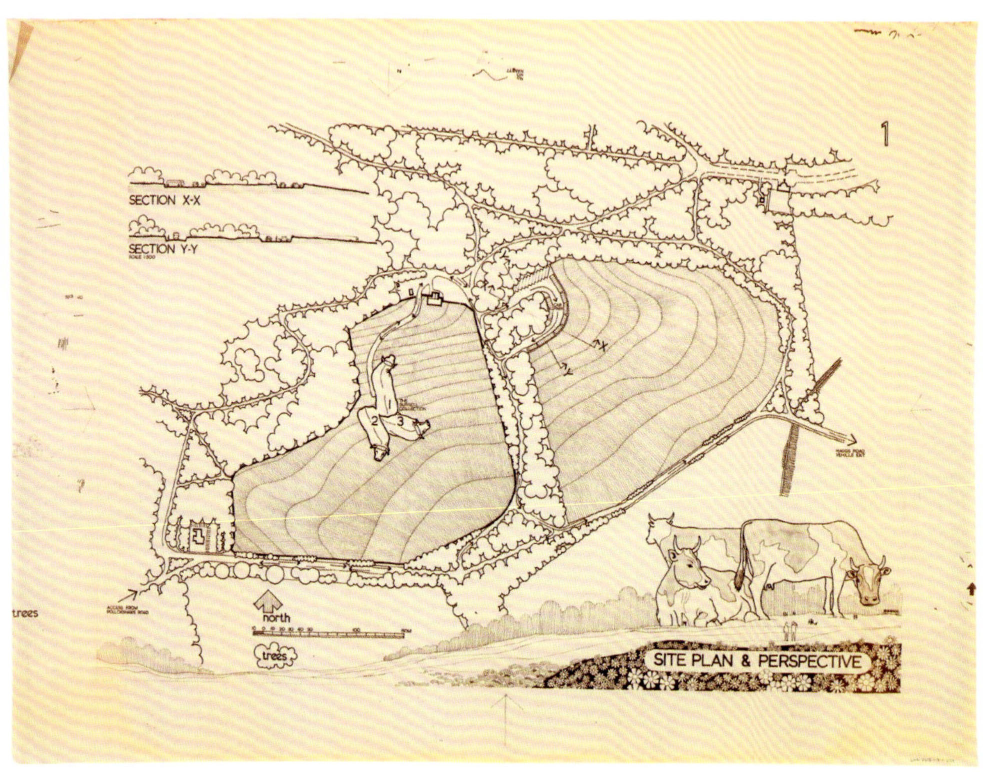

Ray Bryant and Peter Mason, Burrell international architectural competition entry number 050, site plan and perspective, 1970.

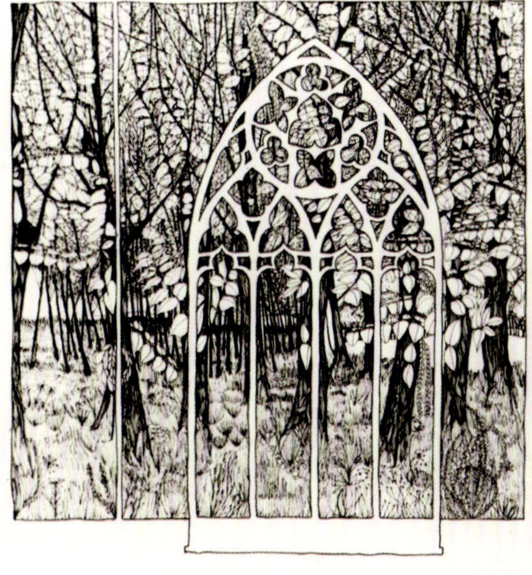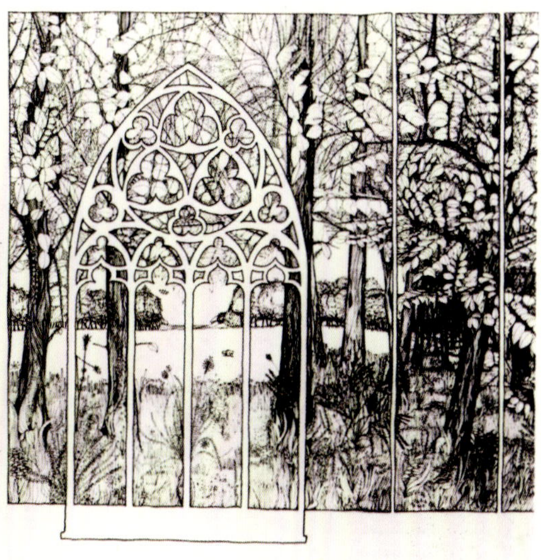

An image from Gasson, Meunier and Andresen's entry number 161, 26 May 1971, showing collection objects at the centre of the design.

A special exhibition was also held at Kelvingrove Art Gallery and Museum, displaying representative objects from, and illustrated books and catalogues on, various parts of the collection.

Despite the brief so emphatically recommending that the design be domestic in scale and respond to the magnificent natural setting, most of the entries were brutalist in style. Monumental forms and exposed concrete were ubiquitous, the proposals clearly influenced by prominent architects of the time such as Le Corbusier and Sir James Stirling (1926–1992), whose work asserted an ideology of utopian brutalism.

Other, more individualistic design entries expressed the wider architectural avant-garde of the epoch. The most notable was a design by Ray Bryant and Peter Mason (opposite), proposing that the collection be housed within aluminium

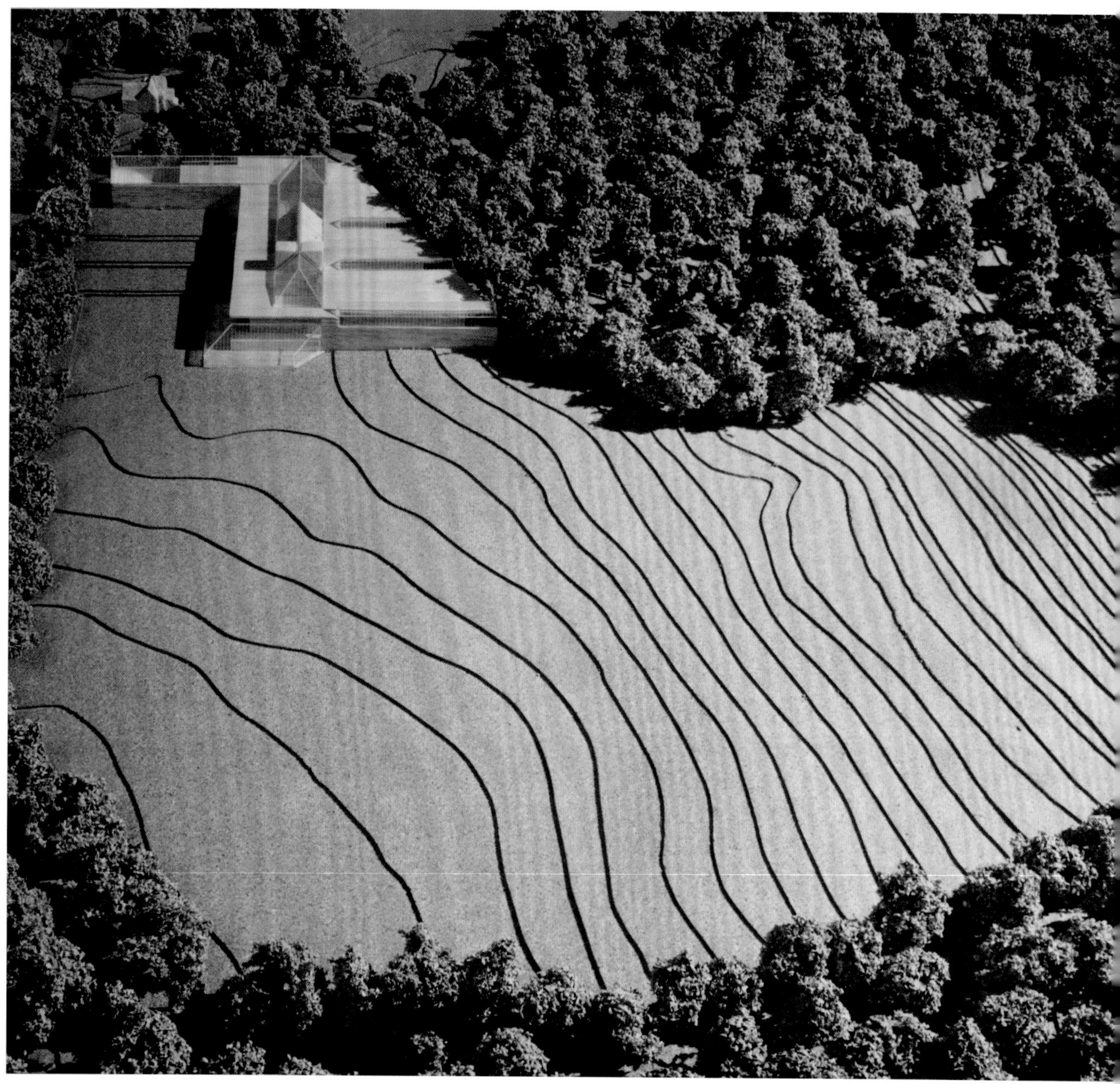

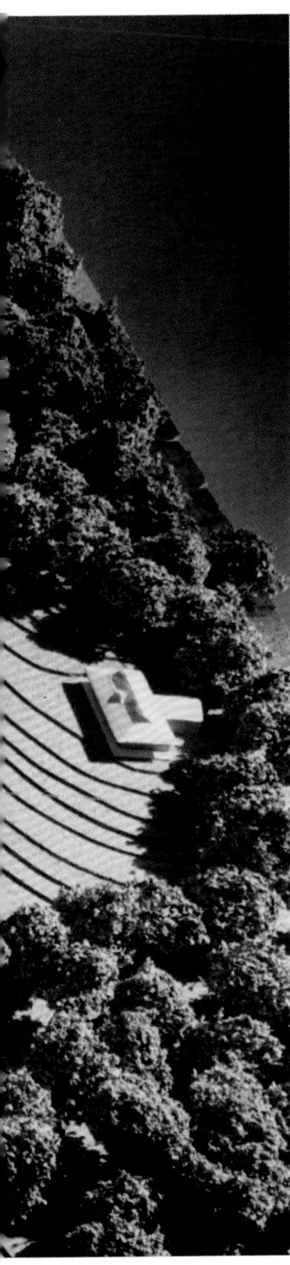

structures in the form of three enormous cows. Whilst this may seem a rather unusual architectural design submission, 'to the Assessors' amazement the entrant's functional interpretation of the brief was very hard to fault!'[11]

At the first stage of the competition, 242 entries were received, of which 175 remain within the Burrell Collection Archives today. These designs provide a fascinating insight into how various architectural practices of the time responded to the same exacting brief and site, and are a great historical snapshot of international architectural theories and trends at the beginning of the 1970s.

Only six submissions reached the final stage of the competition. The remaining entrants submitted more detailed proposals which were publicly exhibited to considerable acclaim before the competition assessors unanimously declared the design by Barry Gasson, John Meunier and Brit Andresen – all then tutors at the University of Cambridge's School of Architecture – as the winner, describing it as 'quite outstanding both in its practicality and its originality and for the way it had been developed in the second stage'.[12]

The Gasson, Meunier and Andresen proposal somewhat uniquely places the building snugly next to the low-level woodland area to the south-west of the site – contextually reticent and neatly coexisting with the mature trees.

Serendipity again played a significant role in this part of the story; Gasson, Meunier and Andresen did not submit their entry on time, and it was only due to a national postal strike and the extension of the deadline that their entry was included.

Historical reports indicate that a perspective drawing by Gasson (see page 21), with collection objects at its centre, and little hint of the architectural design, captured the imagination of the assessors at the first stage of the competition. Another aspect of the design submission that stood out from the others was the location of the building on a predominately sloping and open green space on the lower ground at the west corner of the site; the other entries mostly occupied a much larger portion of the overall site or high ground at the top of the estate. Responding to the existing mature woodland area in that location, this was a modest architectural intervention which, in the spirit of John Stirling Maxwell, respected and protected the surrounding natural landscape and reduced the visual impact of what by necessity would be a large building to a more human scale.

About a year after the announcement of the winning entry in March 1972, Meunier and Andresen had moved on to other architectural positions; Andresen to teach in Australia and Meunier to head the School of Architecture in Cincinnati, leaving Gasson to complete the remaining design and oversee the construction phase to completion.

The original design

'Home' is not a word usually associated with museums, but it is key to the story of the Burrell Collection in that it was central to the location and design of the building, and explicit in Burrell's deed of gift and the competition brief. In his response, Gasson managed to position a civic megastructure at the centre of Pollok Country Park whilst retaining a remarkably domestic scale to the internal spaces. As a result, the vast structure sits perfectly at home in its natural setting, despite all the functional requirements of public access, the space required for such an eclectic collection, and the significant services infrastructure and environmental demands of a museum building.

At the time, Gasson's design was widely recognised as the apogee of architectural structuralism, its lineage traced back to

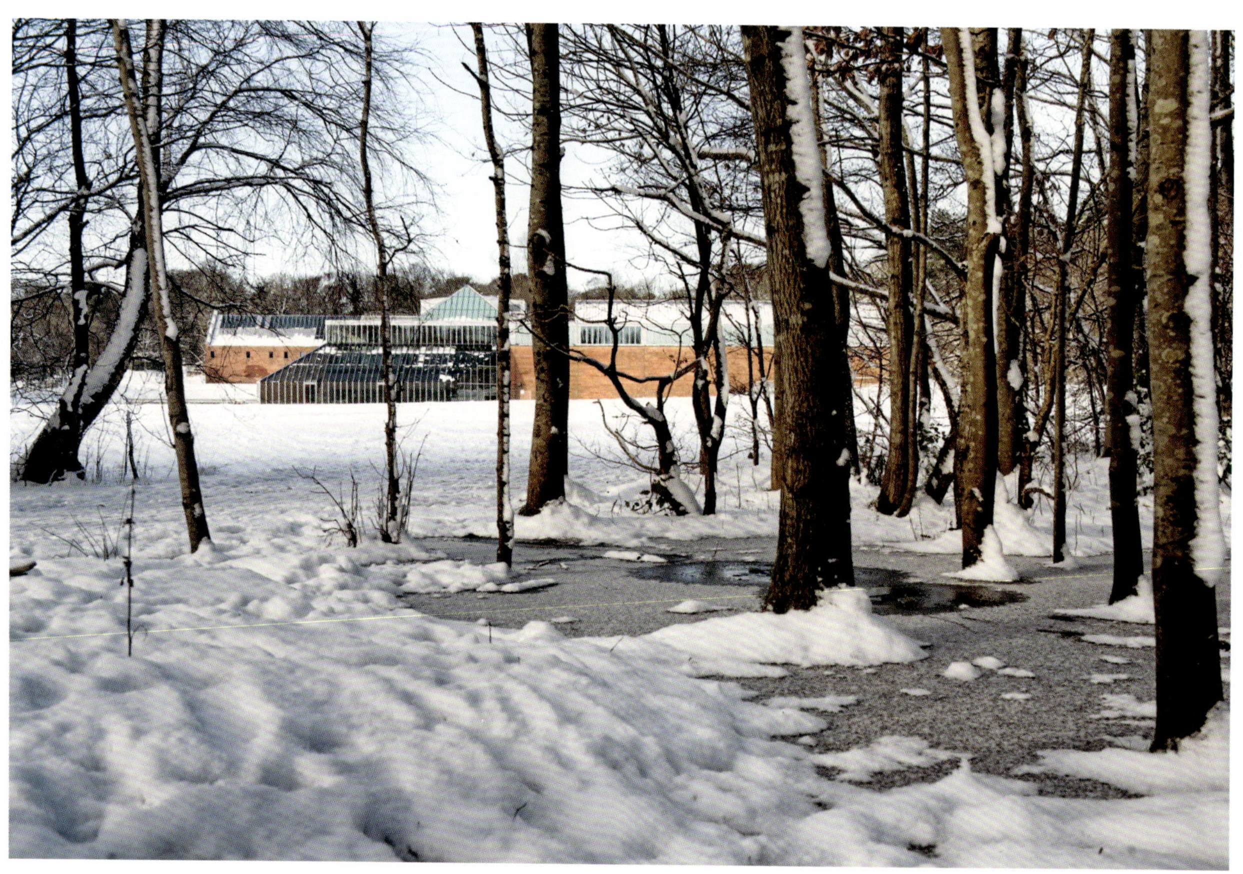

The Burrell Collection nestles within the park.

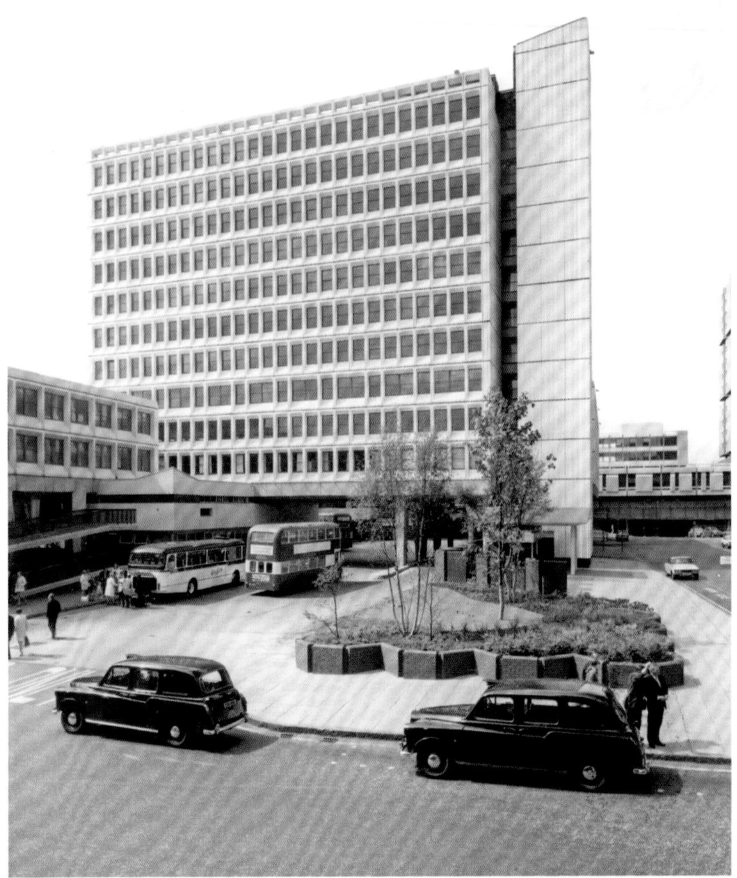

Anderston Cross Commercial Centre in Glasgow city centre, 1972.

and a lifeless expression that ignores the identity of both inhabitants and site context. In design terms, brutalism was also very much seen as an expression of rationalist thought, an example of which was the Anderston Cross Commercial Centre megastructure (now officially branded Cadogan Square) in Glasgow city centre, designed by Richard Seifert (1910–2001) and completed in 1972. In fact, brutalism was the prominent architectural style in Glasgow at this time, in stark contrast to the reticence of Gasson's design.

Rather than a monumental statement, as in brutalist design, Gasson's structuralist ideology was arguably a perfect reply to the brief and site context, but also an approach that aligned with the requirements of the Burrells' gift and the needs of the collection. Creating a symbiotic relationship between visitors, objects and the natural landscape in such a highly sophisticated yet understated way, the original building design bestowed harmony and meaning to the eclectic array of objects for which it was to be home.

the Louisiana Museum of Modern Art near Copenhagen, designed by Jørgen Bo (1919–1999) and Vilhelm Wohlert (1920–2007) in 1958. This design philosophy focused on the building occupants' experience and connection to nature and the landscape – an approach that rejected the elsewhere popular notion of rationalism, which it saw as unhuman

BUILDING A HOME FOR THE COLLECTION

Construction of the building commenced in 1978, overseen by Barry Gasson (b. 1935), who seemed to have so personally embraced Burrell's vision through his detailed design responses and written reports. The works were finally completed in 1983, almost 40 years after the Burrells gifted the collection to the city, and, due to the considerable challenges that needed to be overcome to accommodate one of the world's most remarkable collections, a full 13 years after the launch of the architectural competition.

Inclement weather and rising costs resulting in a funding gap stalled the project, and the late appointment of a conservator and difficulties of fine-tuning the complex mechanical and electrical systems to create the optimal environment for the collection also contributed to the long delivery period.

Whilst much of the success of the competition-winning design had hinged on how effectively it had addressed the far more detailed provisions of the brief at the design development stage, there were still many seemingly contradictory requirements to be met before the proposal could be realised. Gasson's Second Burrell Report highlighted the design challenges he faced, and outlined three principal aims:

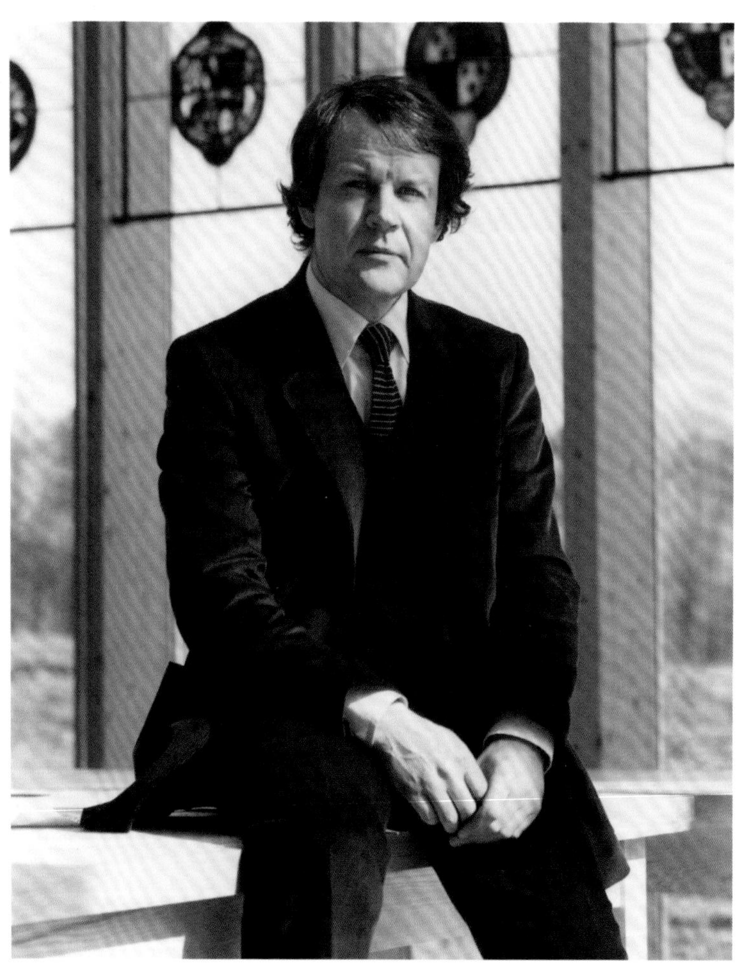

Barry Gasson seated in the Burrell Collection, about 1983.

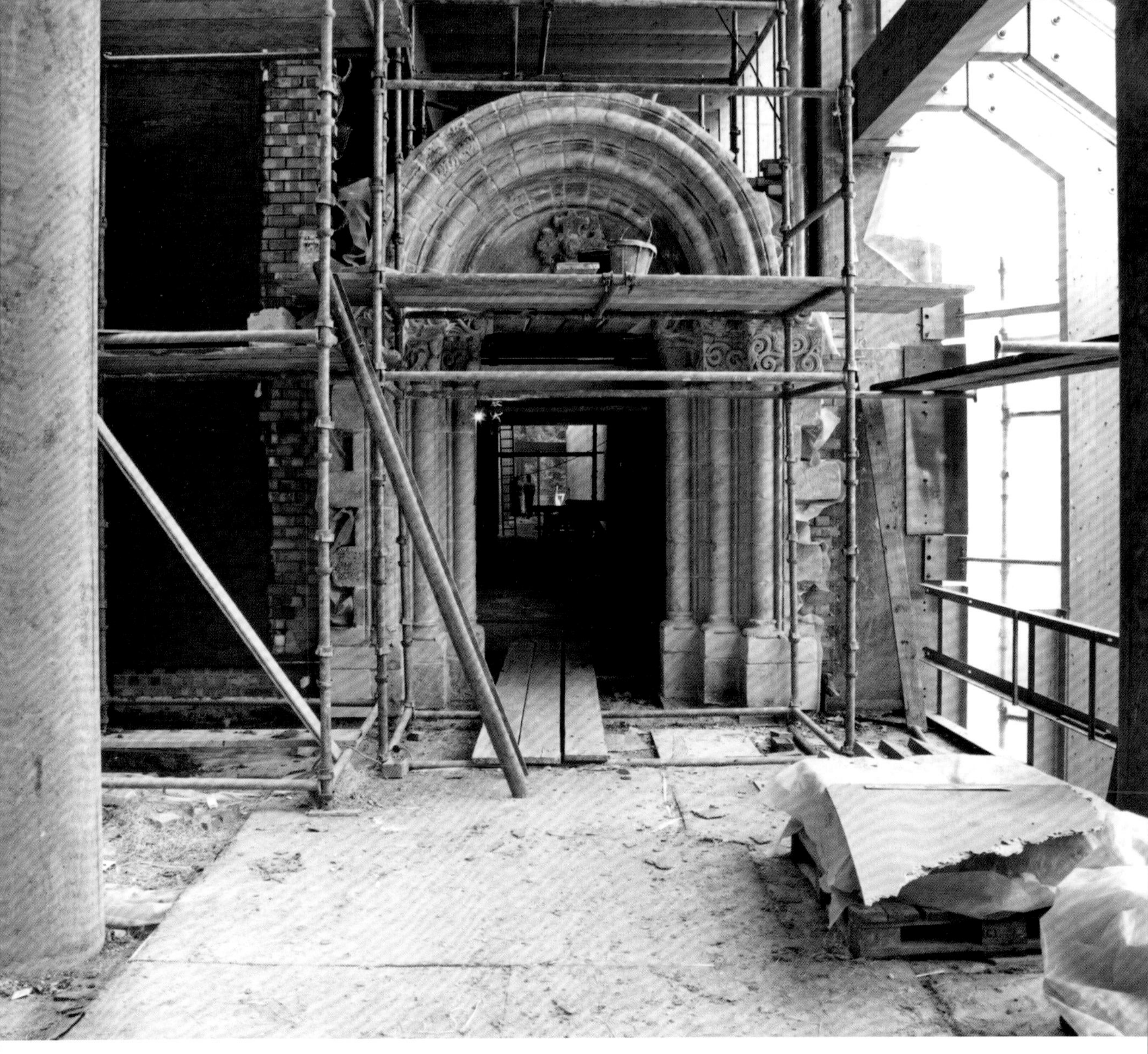

Construction progress
on site, September 1981;
interior door portal.

Firstly, to resolve in the building the conflict between, on the one hand, the rare opportunity of enjoying a superb park, and on the other, the demands of conservation which require that many of the objects in the collection need protection from the light of that outside world. The first requirement tends to make the building open, the second closed, the park offers a context for display, and as such poses the fundamental issue of the relationship between art and nature.

Secondly, to create a variety of opportunities for display; in a Collection of this size there will obviously be a basic order for arranging the objects so that they can be comprehended, yet if there is a selection of places in the building the qualities of place, instead of order might suggest the location of an object. Thus, we hope that we can generate informality and surprise, and that the building will assume some of the characteristics of house as well as museum, which was Sir William Burrell's wish.

Thirdly, to pose the issue of the nature of objects in a museum; how does one display a stone portal, once a doorway and now a piece of sculpture, that was outdoors and is now indoors? What is a piece of stained glass that once had a location and message, and now has history and is preserved forever? How does one display objects of one epoch in a building that denies many of the qualities of that epoch? How does one resolve the relationship of objects that are very explicit in themselves to a building that tends not to be?[13]

Here, Gasson also seemed to be beginning to identify some of the opportunities and challenges presented by the site itself.

Site Plan

1. Entrance
2. Cloakrooms
3. Courtyard
4. Shop sales
5. Italian-style courtyard and Warwick Vase
6. Burrells' Hutton Drawing Room
7. Burrells' Hutton Hall
8. Burrells' Hutton Dining Room
9. North Gallery 'walk in the woods'
10. North Gallery short / long corridors
11. Central Galleries
12. East Galleries
13. Temporary exhibition gallery
14. Lecture theatre
15. South Galleries
16. Restaurant
17. Landscaped terrace
18. Sloping green space
19. Woodland

● Hornby Arch
● Warwick Vase
● Hornby Portal

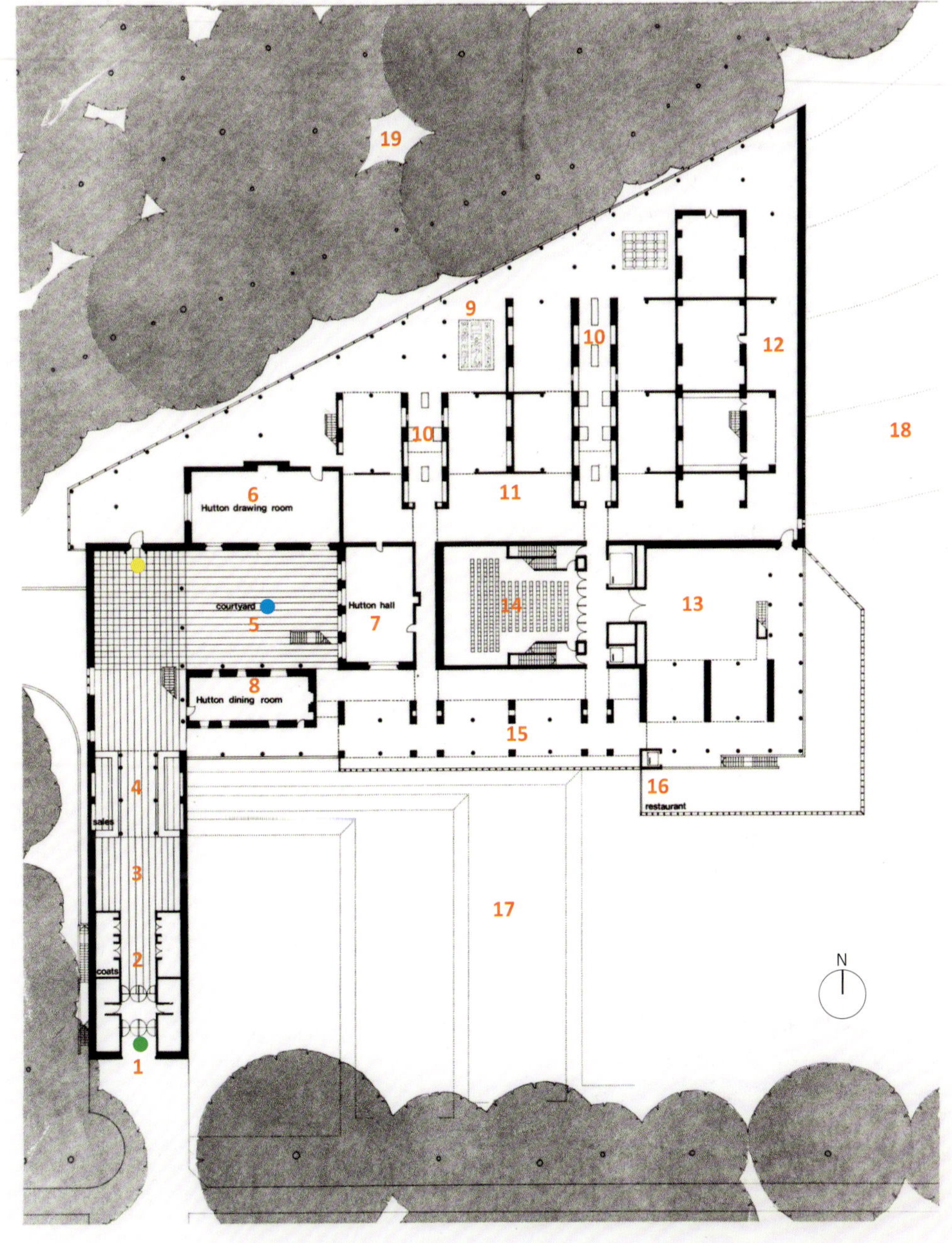

19
9
10
12
10
11
18
6
Hutton drawing room
courtyard
5
Hutton hall
7
14
13
8
Hutton dining room
15
16
restaurant
sales
4
3
coats
2
1
17
N

Visitor experience

To understand in more detail how Gasson's original design for the building epitomised the collection's ideology, it is helpful to look at how it was intended to be accessed and experienced. Its symbiotic relationship with the collection and the landscape was highly choreographed, the building merely providing the backdrop to the story of the objects, with moments of deviation to the external scenery.

The visitor journey begins with a large volume of red ashlar sandstone reaching out from the main body of the building, into which is built an ornate medieval stone arch from the collection, the Hornby Arch, which signifies the architectural intent to highlight the objects within. It conjures thoughts of a church entrance, perhaps a symbolic gesture representing the ideas of the Renaissance enlightenment, with the modern museum replacing the church. Crossing the medieval stone threshold, the journey continues through a series of small utility spaces to Gasson's Italian-style courtyard garden, where large, glazed canopies provide an abundance of light from above, also invoking a modern, cathedral-like space. Fittingly, here can be found the second-century Warwick Vase, from the gardens of the Roman Emperor Hadrian, acquired by the Burrell Trustees specifically for display within the building. Adjacent to the courtyard are the extensive volumes of the gallery spaces, which are announced by a grand, sixteenth-century English archway, the Hornby Portal, which emphasises the next phase of the journey to meet the collection objects.

Gasson's plan was far removed from a traditional neoclassical museum, providing a visitor journey that emphasises the drama and surprise of crossing thresholds and connection to and orientation with both the objects and the landscape through vistas and focal points that change according to different times of the day and season.

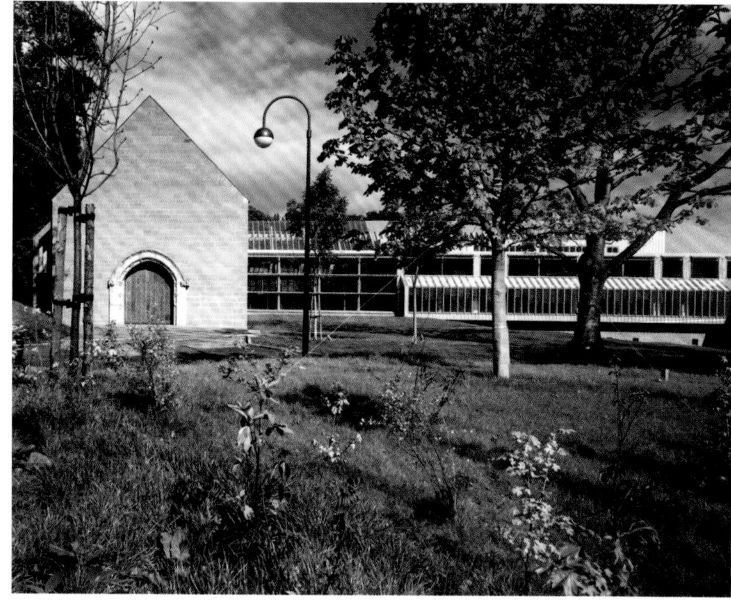

The original entrance with the Hornby Arch prior to the building alterations. Photograph Keith Gibson.

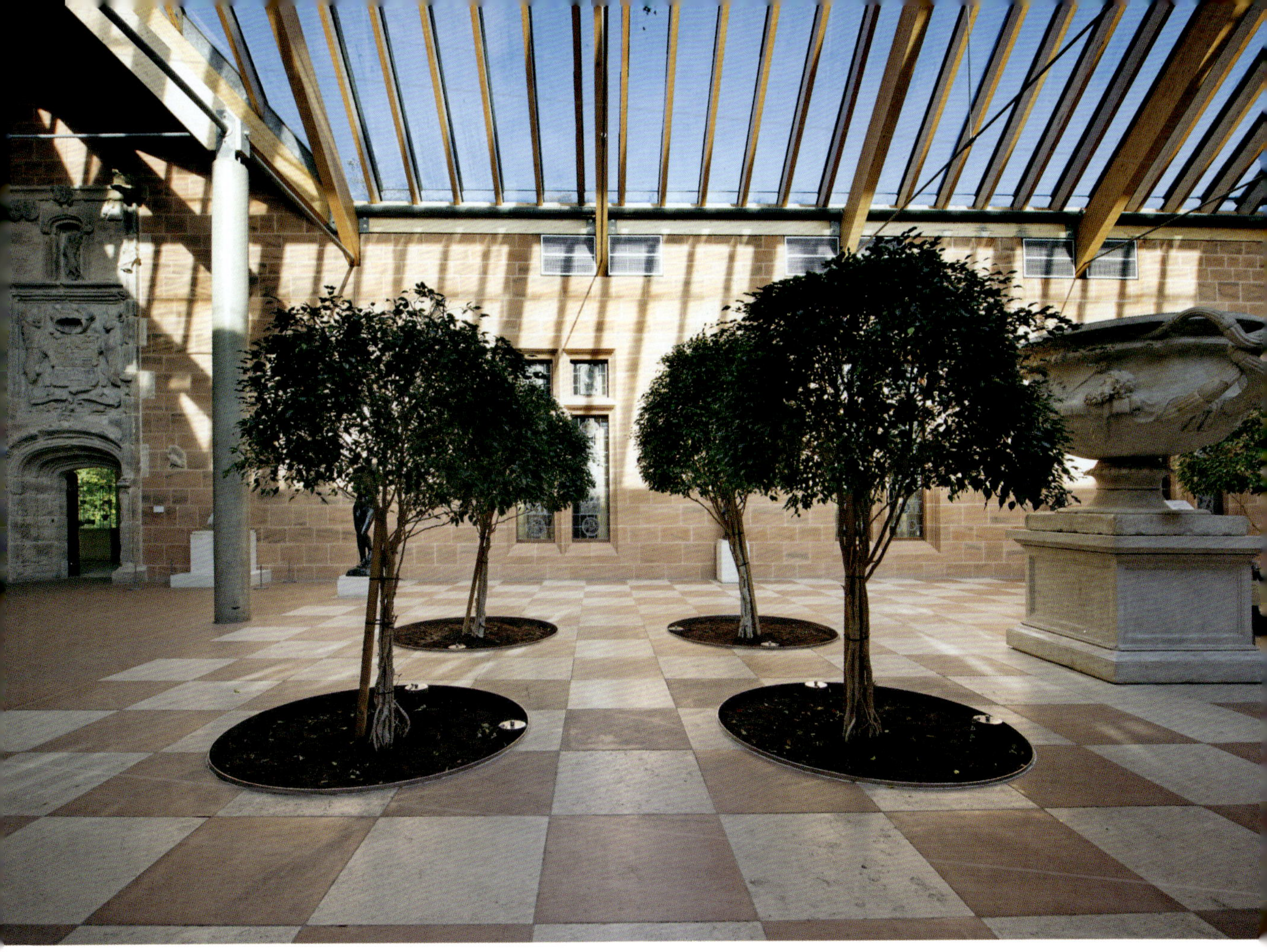

Gasson's Italian-style courtyard and the Hornby Portal in 2016.

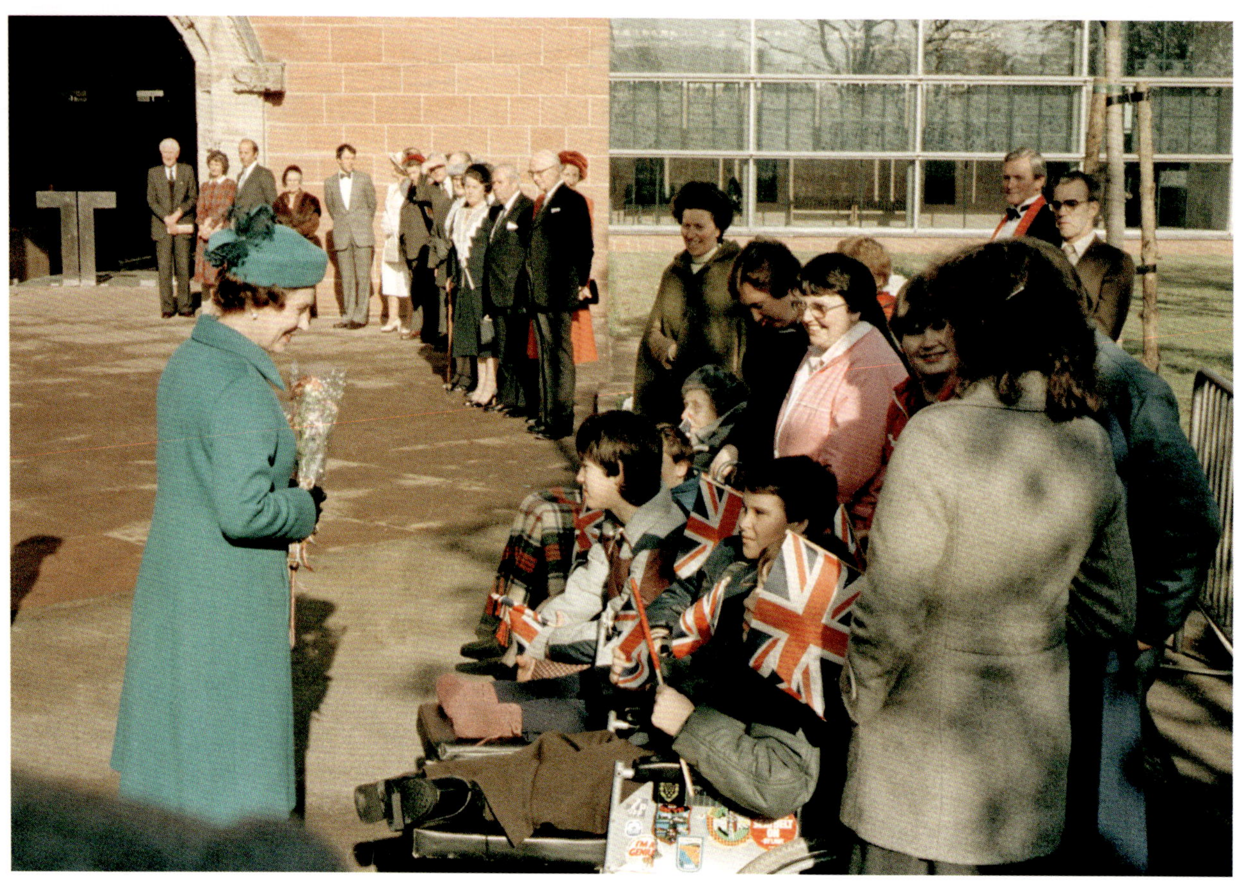

Official opening of the
Burrell Collection by
Queen Elizabeth II,
21 October 1983.

A cultural renaissance

The Burrell Collection was formally opened by Queen Elizabeth II in 1983, representing an important milestone in the cultural renaissance and reinvention of Glasgow during the 1980s and 1990s, as well as a shift in its international reputation. In the months leading up to the opening, the city launched the 'Glasgow's Miles Better' marketing campaign. In her opening speech the Queen remarked that 'visitors would flock to Pollok Park from all over the world, to see for themselves the warm smile of Glasgow's face'. The *New York Times* ran with 'Glasgow's Treasures Belie its Gritty Image', the *Globe and Mail* with 'It isn't Grim Glasgow Anymore', and the *Wall Street Journal* 'Glasgow Cleans Up Its Act – With Art'.[14]

A series of other cultural events followed over the next two decades, the most notable of which included the Glasgow Garden Festival (1988), a cultural regeneration of a large area of derelict land in a former industrial district which was later developed into what is now known as the Glasgow Science Centre, and the city's designation as European Capital of Culture in 1990 then City of Architecture and Design in 1999, providing further building blocks for its culture-led urban regeneration.

The city, as well as a generation of Scotland's architects, artists and designers, was once again growing in confidence on the world stage, initiated and inspired by the completion of the Burrell Collection. This was a model later duplicated in other cities around the world, and most notably in Bilbao, Spain. However, although Glasgow hosted a delegation from Bilbao who came to learn about the Burrell project, such culture-led regeneration is now often referred to as the 'Bilbao Effect'.

Major building projects in the city were to follow, including the Scottish Exhibition and Conference Centre (Foster + Partners, 1985), Kelvin Hall International Sports Arena (City of Glasgow District Council, Department of Architecture and Related Services, 1988), Glasgow Royal Concert Hall (Sir Leslie Martin, 1990), Gallery of Modern Art (City of Glasgow District Council, Department of Architecture and Related Services, 1996), the refurbishment of Kelvingrove Art Gallery and Museum (BDP, 2006), and the Riverside Museum of Transport (Zaha Hadid Architects, 2011).

The Coca-Cola Roller at the Glasgow Garden Festival, August 1988. The Finnieston Crane, a reminder of the city's shipbuilding past, can be seen in the distance. Colour slide taken by Glasgow street photographer Eric Watt.

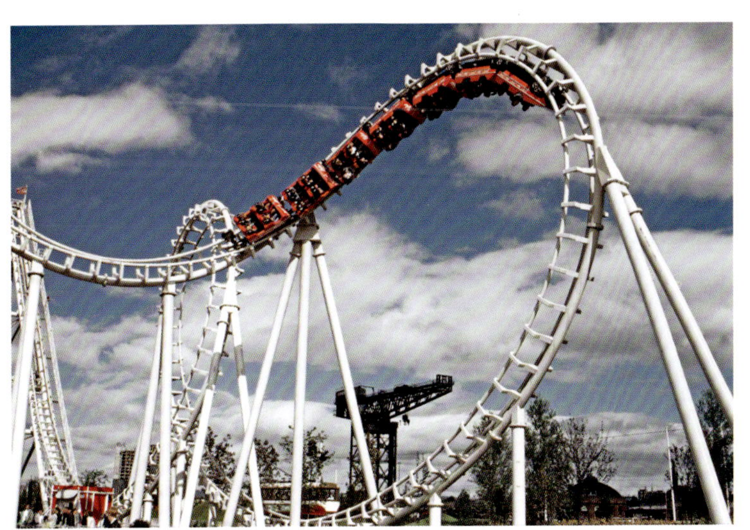

THE NEED FOR REFURBISHMENT

The Burrell Collection opened to much public and academic acclaim, and won the prestigious National Heritage Museum of the Year award in 1985 (now the Art Fund Museum of the Year), receiving the trophy *Moon Head*, by Henry Moore. The *Architects' Journal* published a substantial review to coincide with the royal opening.[15] The significance was captured on the front cover with the title 'Barry's Burrell Gallery: Special Report'. The journal devoted 34 pages to the Burrell, including five essays and four personal viewpoints. It is a fascinating read as it captures contemporary thinking during a period of much architectural transition and uncertainty. However, for the Burrell, the essay by Richard Demarco, Scottish artist and promoter of visual and performing arts, stands out, as it seems to have encapsulated a more holistic view of the contributors' as well as his own thoughts on Gasson's design ethos:

> *It is becoming increasingly obvious that without the most vital ingredient, art – despite the advanced technology at our disposal – the contemporary built environment, particularly of our large towns and cities such as Glasgow, cannot last until the year 2000. Human nature is bound to reject any man-made structures that represent a merely materialistic or utilitarian function.*
>
> *Art exists to remind us that we cannot live by bread alone.*[16]

The publication leaves an indelible legacy for the Burrell, providing a rich written source of art and architectural heritage reference material that informed the briefing and design ethos of the recent refurbishment and will no doubt direct future renovations.

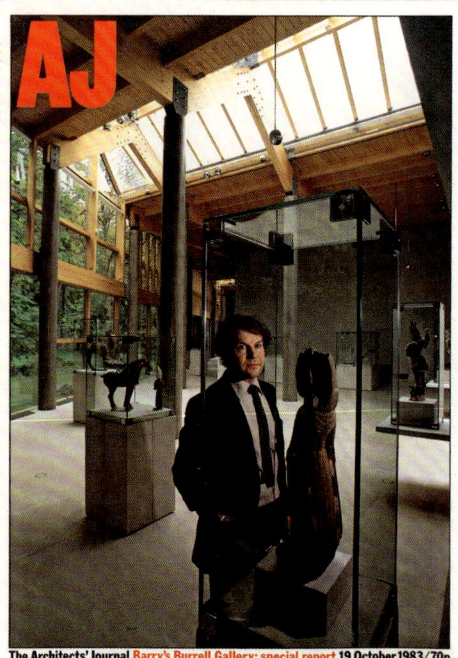

Front cover, *Architects' Journal*, 19 October 1983, showing Barry Gasson in the Burrell Collection.

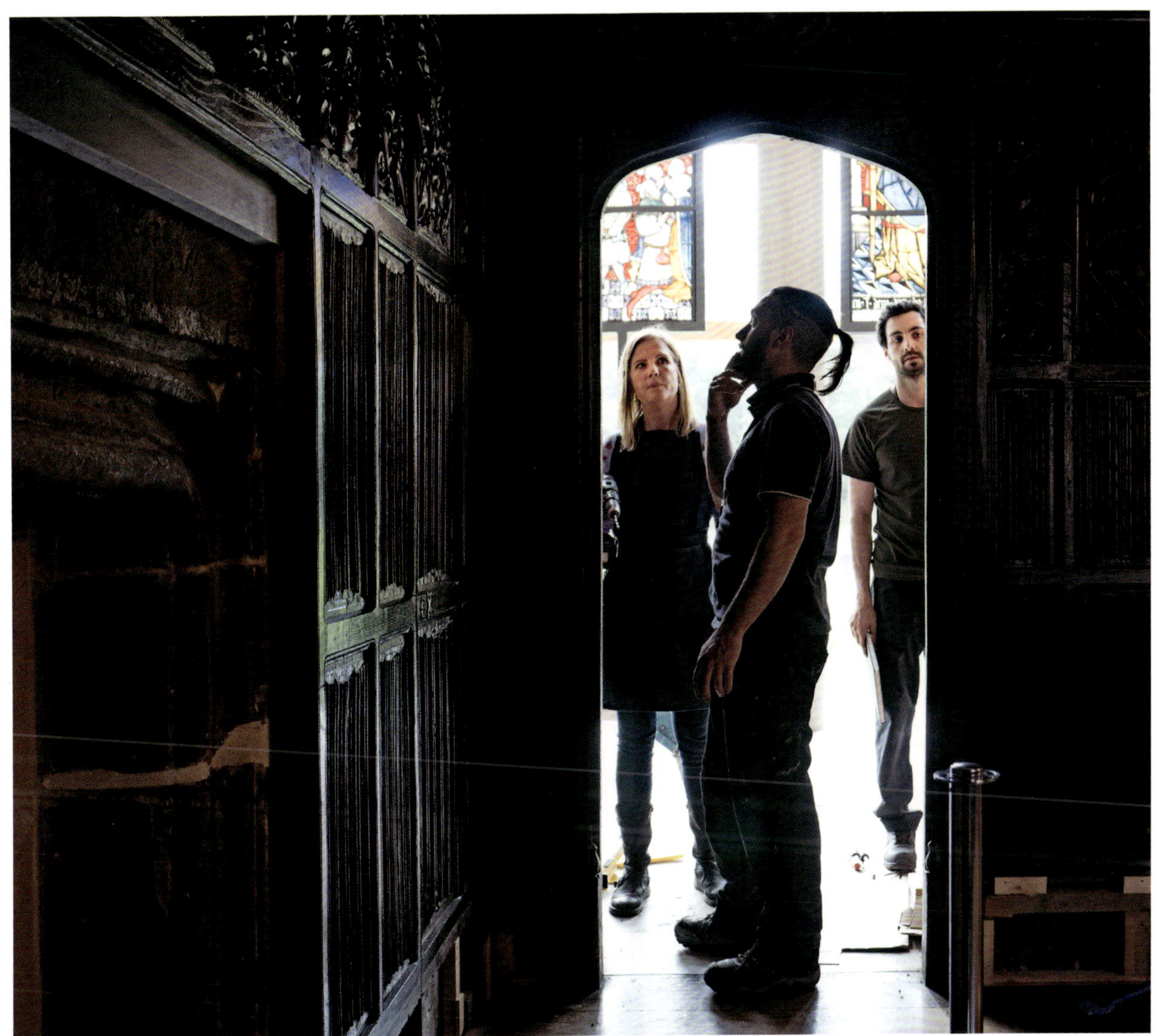

Conservators preparing to remove accessioned wall panelling during the object decant.

The museum collection

The way the objects were displayed had not changed since the museum first opened to the public in 1983, and interpretation methods had changed significantly in the intervening years, including the increased use of digital technologies and interactive elements. Additionally, the object cases did not meet modern museum standards – there was no display lighting, and the tinted glass obscured the objects, but most importantly they provided very little environmental protection, placing the artefacts themselves at risk.

Building fabric

After 40 years, what had been the very latest in modern building technologies at the time were deteriorating. Leaks in the roof were becoming increasingly more frequent, requiring continual vigilance on the part of staff to ensure temporary interventions were implemented to protect the collection. Above all, a major overhaul of the external fabric was required to improve the environmental performance of the building envelope.

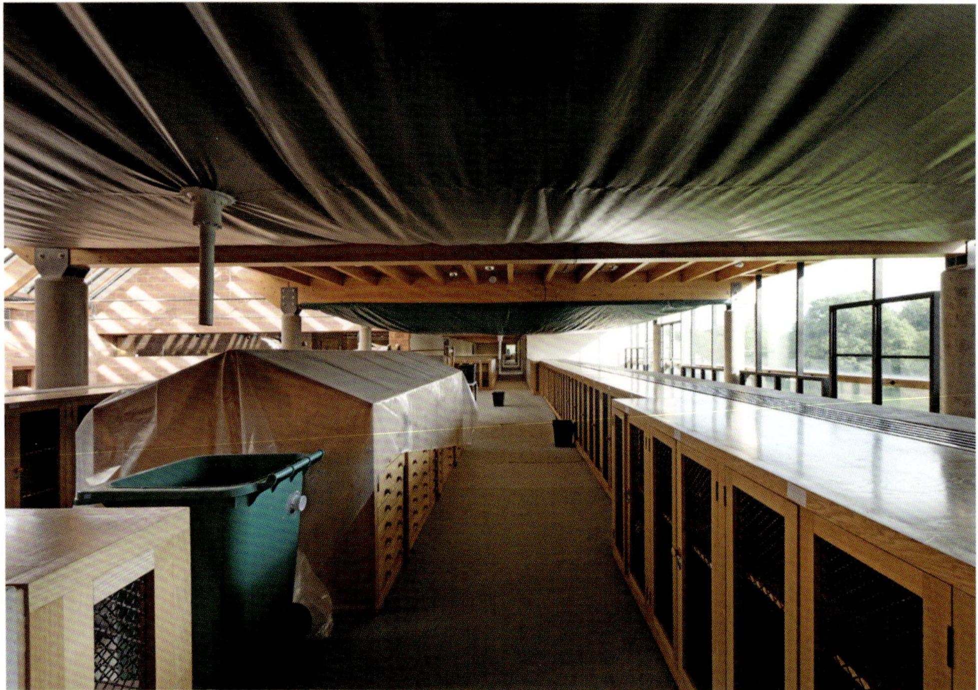

Sheets of polythene covering cabinets, protecting against water ingress prior to building upgrading work.

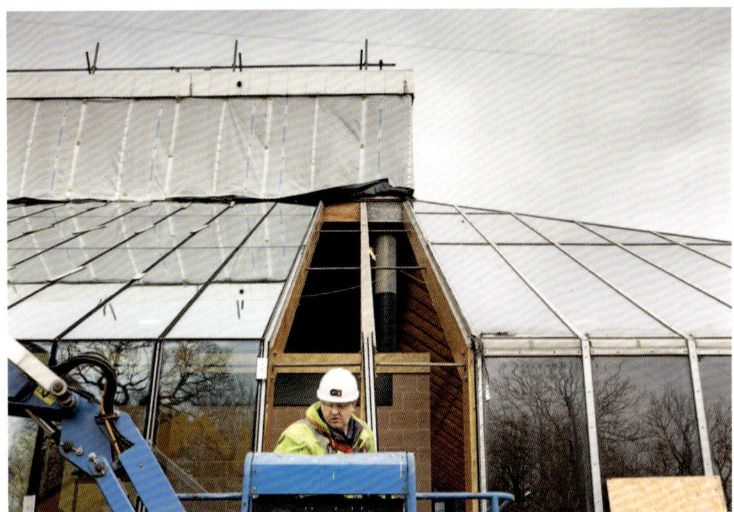

A contractor upgrades the glazing on the exterior of the building fabric.

Access and orientation

Since the Burrell first opened, visitor expectations of major attractions have changed. Visitor research studies and access audits undertaken by Glasgow Life Museums highlighted many issues with access and orientation throughout the building and only very limited provision of accessible facilities. To ensure better access and wider inclusivity, substantial interventions were required to remove barriers and provide additional accessible support facilities to enhance the visitor experience.

Building services and environmental conditions

The building's engineering services had become old and inefficient, resulting in reduced environmental control and comfort for both building occupants and the collection. The combination of a degenerating building fabric envelope and inefficient plant had also resulted in unsustainably high energy costs. A complete replacement of the services infrastructure was required to reduce energy consumption and ensure that the internal environment would be suitable for museum visitors and museum objects.

Plant in the Burrell Collection prior to the building upgrading.

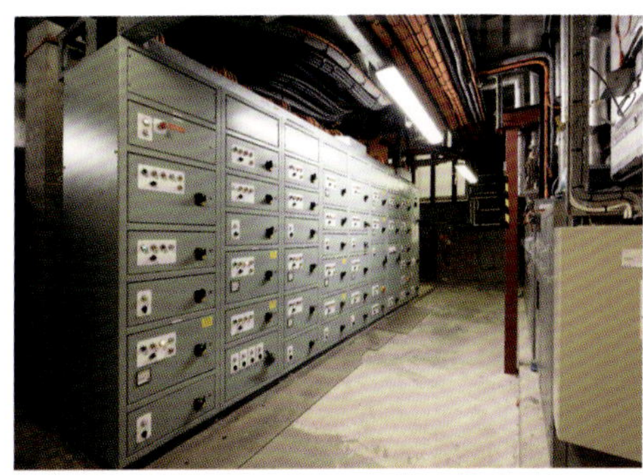

Community engagement

Glaswegians have a special relationship with their city's collections of art and artefacts – a real sense of ownership and pride. Free access to the collections is not only deeply rooted culturally and politically but is a legal condition, which recognises that Glasgow's cultural assets belong to its citizens. For the Burrell Collection to have a meaningful and sustainable future, Glasgow Life Museums understood that key to the success of the refurbishment would be meeting the needs and aspirations of local people, ensuring the building would remain a key place for the community to meet and enjoy a day out, and also offer space for personal learning and reflection. The project would need to carefully weave together and maintain the stipulations and aspirations of what came before to ensure the ongoing safety and care of the collection but at the same time meet the needs of modern users.

An extensive consultation programme including interviews, focus groups, surveys, prototype testing and work with a range of Glasgow Life Museums advisory panels involved engaging with more than 15,000 local people of all ages, who provided new ideas, opinions and fresh insights which informed the refurbishment brief and decision-making process throughout the project. The residents of Glasgow have a tradition not only of great pride in their city, but also of being vocal in their defence of it. Harnessing this was central to the success of the building redesign, including the new gallery displays and the learning and community spaces.

One Glasgow Life Museums' staff member who was involved in carrying out research as part of the Visitor Studies team commented that she had been 'constantly amazed by the enthusiasm and love for the Burrell Collection demonstrated by the public when we asked them to participate in our research. Visitors are excited that their thoughts and opinions have helped shape the project and have willingly participated in evaluation, surveys and product testing.'[17]

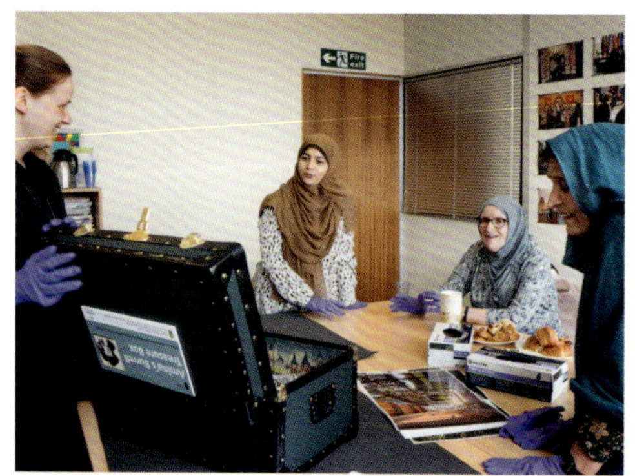

Local residents from Amina – The Muslim Women's Resource Centre – developing an educational object-handling box with Glasgow Life Museums staff.

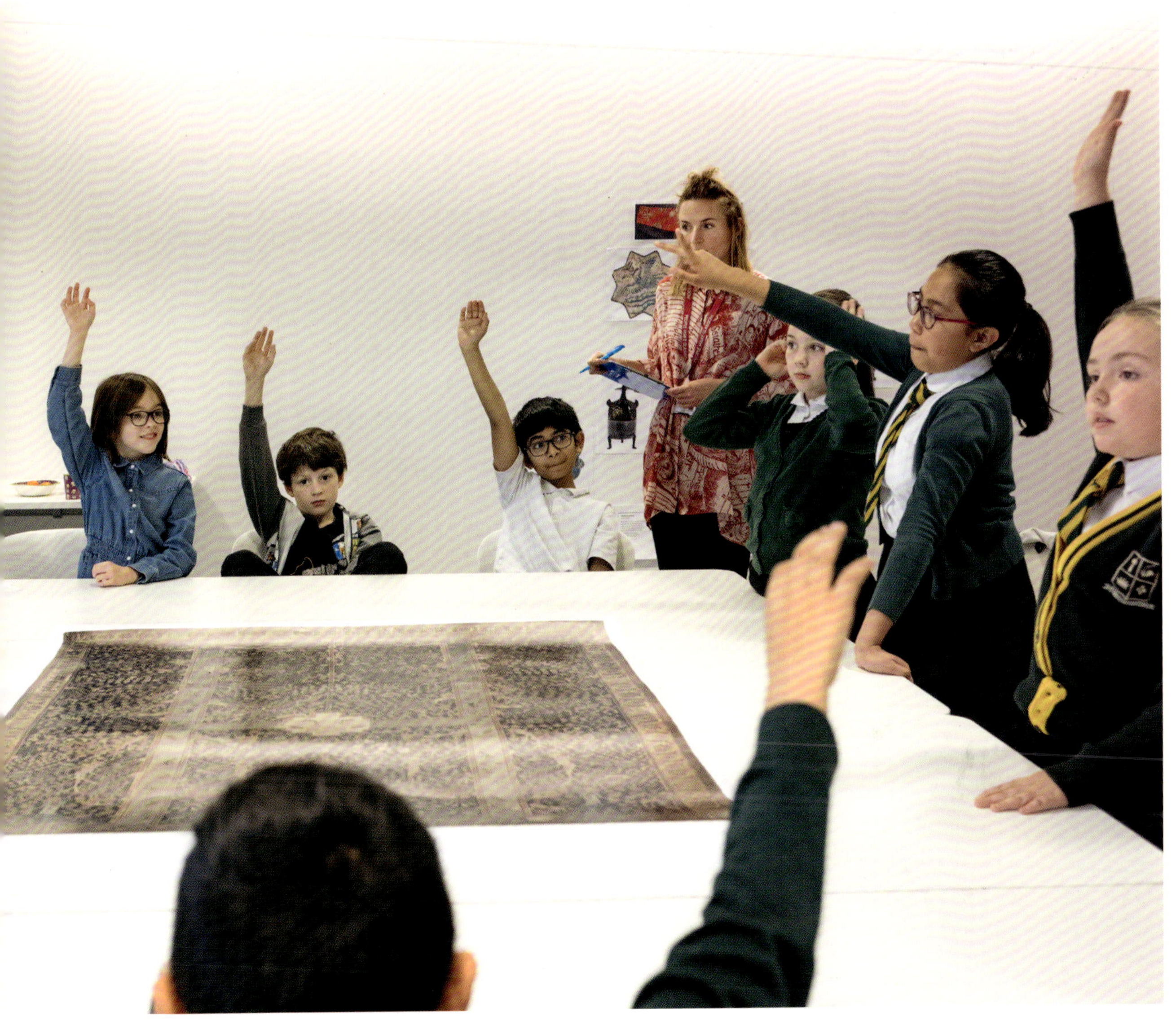

Focus testing with the
Schools Advisory
Panel, 2019.

THE MASTERPLAN AND ARCHITECTURAL BRIEF

In February 2013, in advance of the refurbishment, the building was assessed by Historic Environment Scotland and given a Category A listing, recognising that it is of international significance. This is rare for a postmodernist building, but more notable and even more unusual is that the display cases – non-building elements – were included in the listing. This had a significant effect on the refurbishment project brief and the design process, as the building and the display cases were now legally protected from alterations and subject to detailed statutory assessment by conservation and heritage professionals.

The main challenge was to deliver the original intent for the building while retaining its key aesthetic qualities, and to create a new model of how the building would operate and perform in a sustainable way into the future.

The objectives identified included the creation of an inspirational international museum as well as a proud community venue; broadening visitation by increasing public access to the collection, and removing physical, social and economic barriers; and minimising energy consumption and achieving significant reductions in CO_2 emissions using a building 'fabric first' approach, heat-recovery techniques and low- and zero-carbon technologies along with a sustainable operating model. In addition, it would need to be a 'connected museum' that recognised its parkland setting, with wider environmental improvements including the delivery of an Active and Sustainable Travel plan with upgraded access routes, solar photovoltaic panels supplying power for a free electric park bus, community planting of native bluebells and new indigenous tree planting.

The brief specified that the refurbishment proposals must include the renovation of the roof and the re-glazing of the building with high-performance solar-control glass. A combination of improvements to the fabric, the mechanical and electrical installations, energy management and the provision of on-site renewable energy were needed to support the aim of reducing carbon emissions. To tackle the problems of orientation, circulation and restricted access, a new main entrance was envisaged at ground-floor level as well as a new café entrance. It was also proposed that the administrative and ancillary spaces on the upper floors be removed to provide more public and gallery space. A new learning and community space was to be included, as well as a new shop and improved café facilities. All of which

Event Communications' initial concept sketch for the development of a Central Hub and staircase.

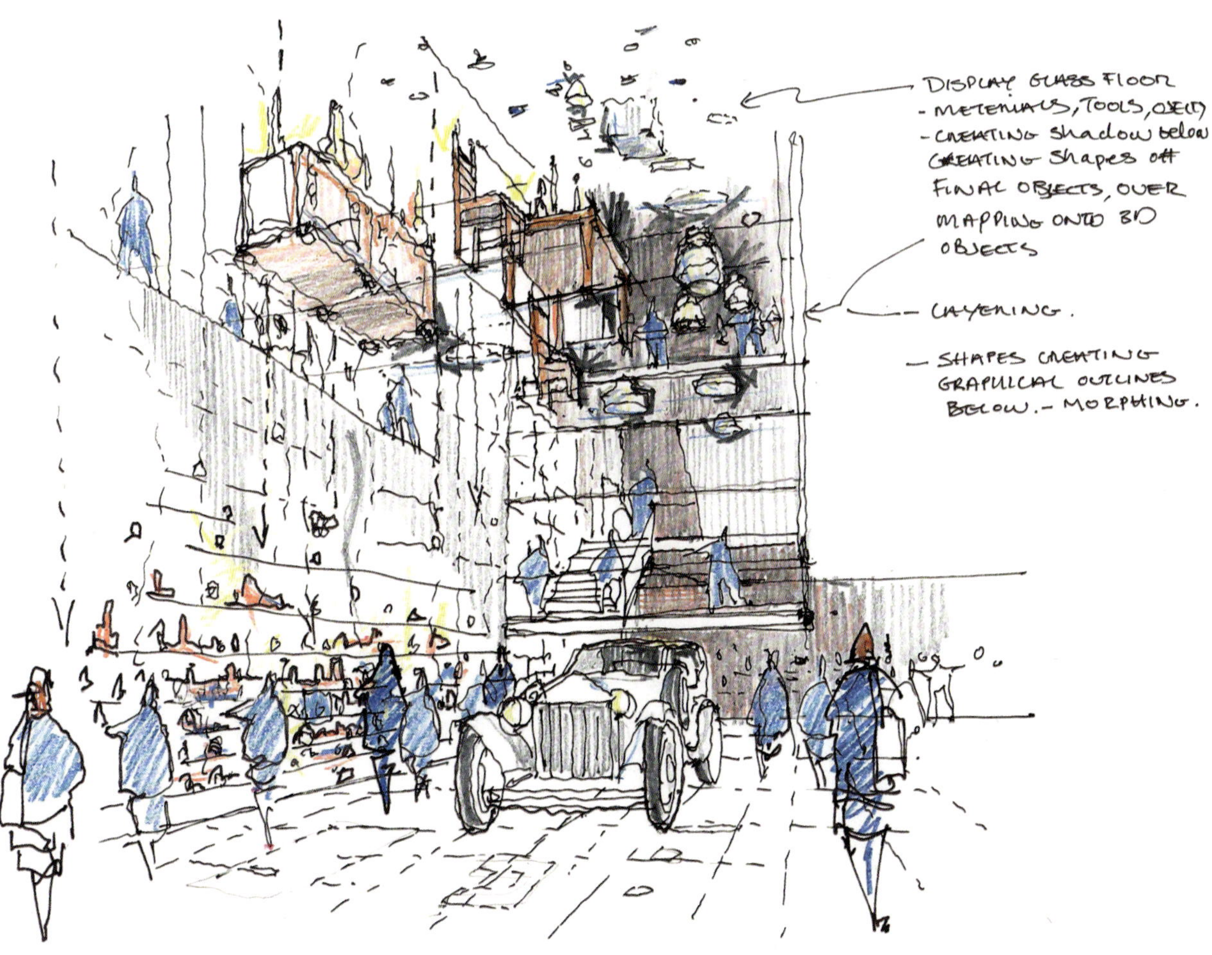

DISPLAY GLASS FLOOR
- MATERIALS, TOOLS, USED
- CREATING SHADOW BELOW
CREATING SHAPES OF
FINAL OBJECTS, OVER
MAPPING ONTO 3D
OBJECTS

- LAYERING.

- SHAPES CREATING
GRAPHICAL OUTLINES
BELOW. - MORPHING.

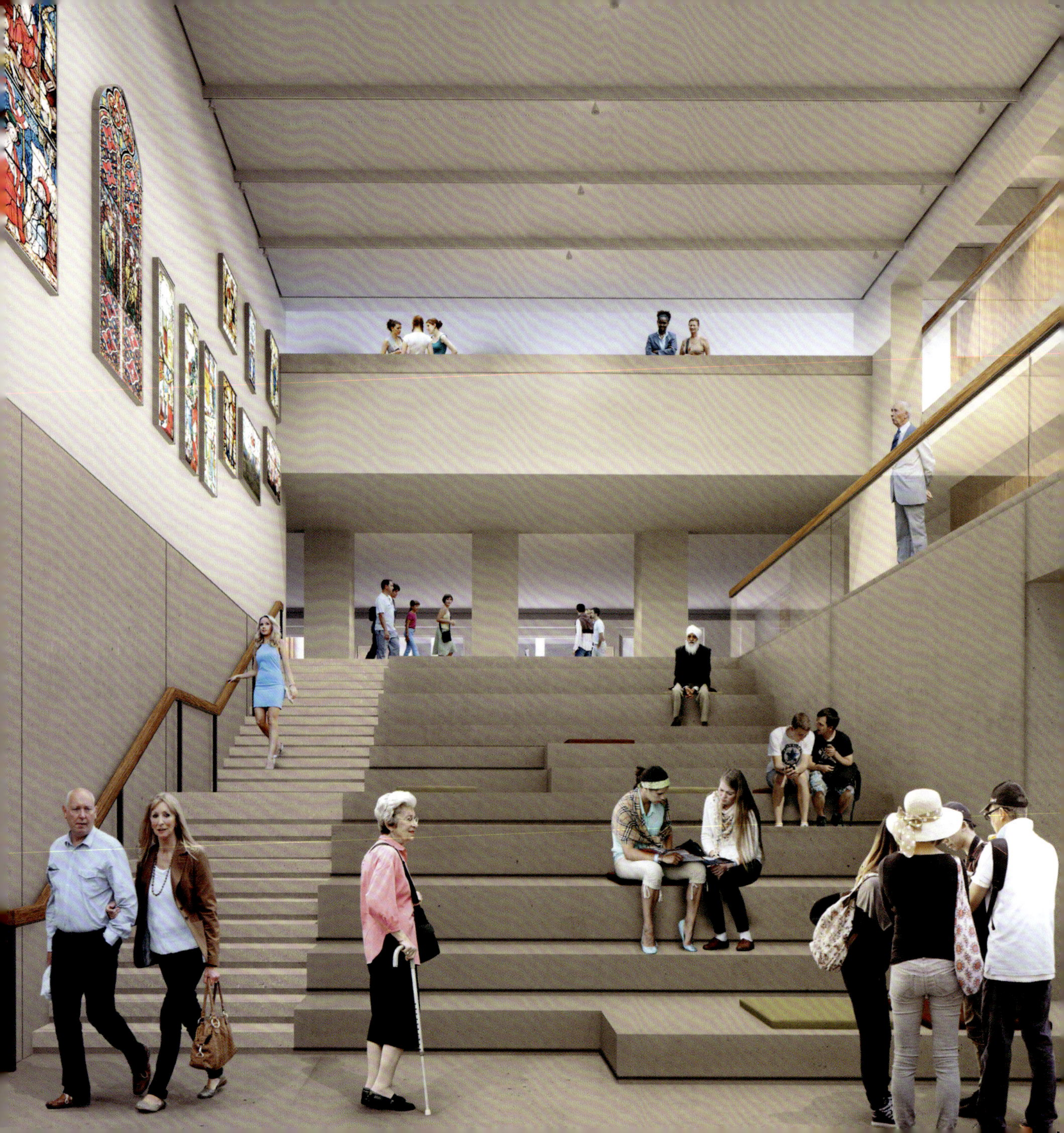

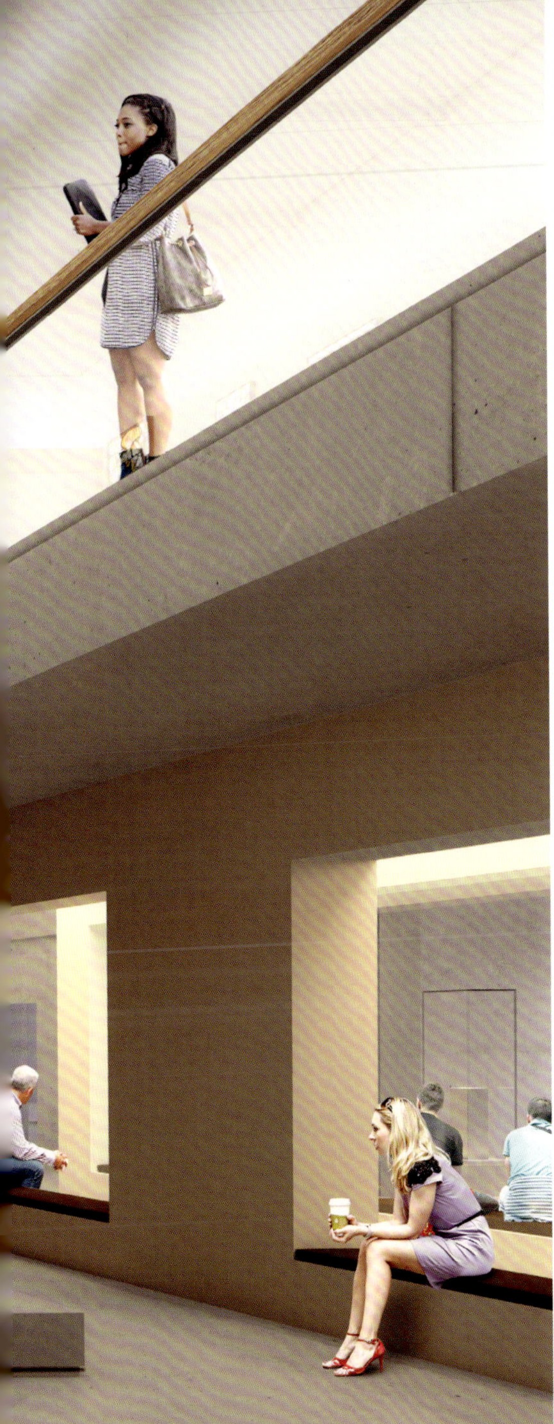

John McAslan's artistic visualisation of the three-level Central Hub and staircase.

needed to maintain the spirit of the Burrell Collection.

In 2014, Event Communications – one of Europe's longest established museum and visitor attraction design practices – was appointed to work with Glasgow Life Museums to develop a redevelopment and redisplay masterplan, informed by the extensive public engagement and research process that had already been carried out. This established the foundations and main aims of the project as well as the detailed development brief and key outcomes.

Glasgow City Council then appointed project managers Gardiner & Theobald along with architects John McAslan + Partners (who had prepared an initial architectural study in 2012 that informed the masterplan and briefing) to lead a multidisciplinary design team to deliver the architectural brief, with Event Communications remaining responsible for the delivery of the galleries and interpretative design.

Born in Glasgow, John McAslan (b. 1954) represented the start of a new architectural chapter in the story of the Burrell Collection, and brought to the project both the local and international experience that was required for such a prominent refurbishment. In response to the brief, his practice's design approach involved a combination of significant but sensitive architectural interventions to the internal spaces and some more delicate and sophisticated touches – all conceived to create new visitor journeys through new spaces whilst avoiding any dilution of, or disruption to, Gasson's original architectural philosophy.

NEW JOURNEYS AND NEW SPACES

The visitor journey has always been an important aspect of the Burrell Collection experience, and today it begins with a woodland walk (or free park bus) through Pollok Country Park towards a curated entrance, before continuing through a procession of internal public spaces and galleries. Internally, the use of vistas back over the park setting provides moments to pause and step away from collection interpretation, reminding visitors not only of the building's natural surroundings, but also of the connection of the objects to the landscape. This original Gasson idea remained a key theme in McAslan's approach.

Gasson's original scheme offered a single access and egress point to which visitors were directed via footpaths from the car park or nearby train station. Formal external landscaping was limited to a small, paved area in front of the building and the approach was therefore very clearly defined. There were good reasons for this at the time – primarily to limit openings in the building envelope

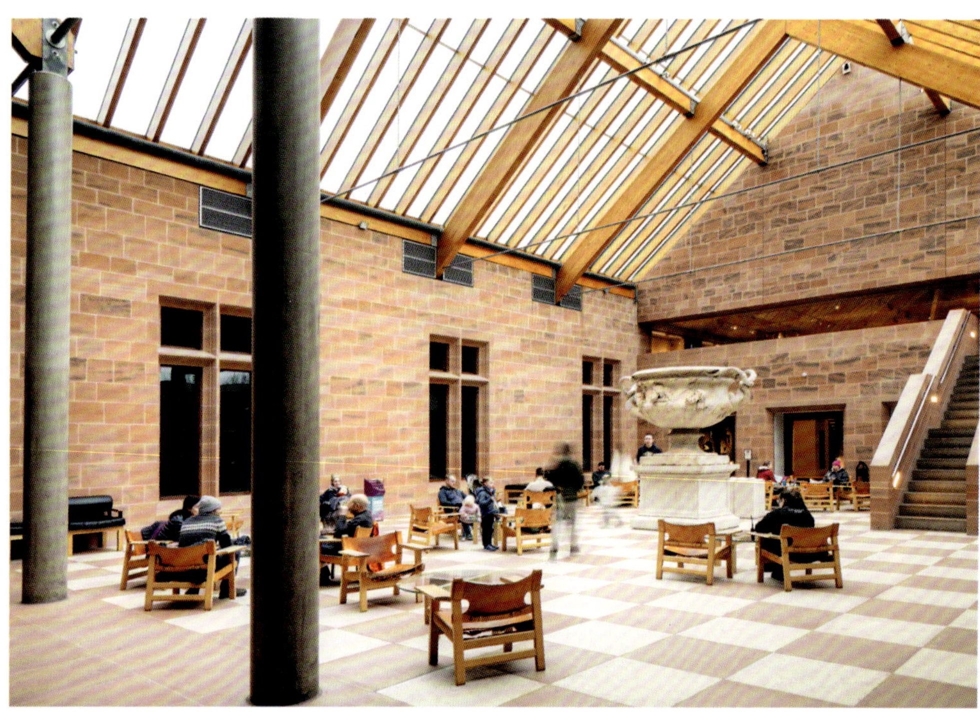

Gasson's Italian-style courtyard and the Warwick Vase, looking towards one of the former Hutton Rooms, now a display on the Burrells in Glasgow, 2025.

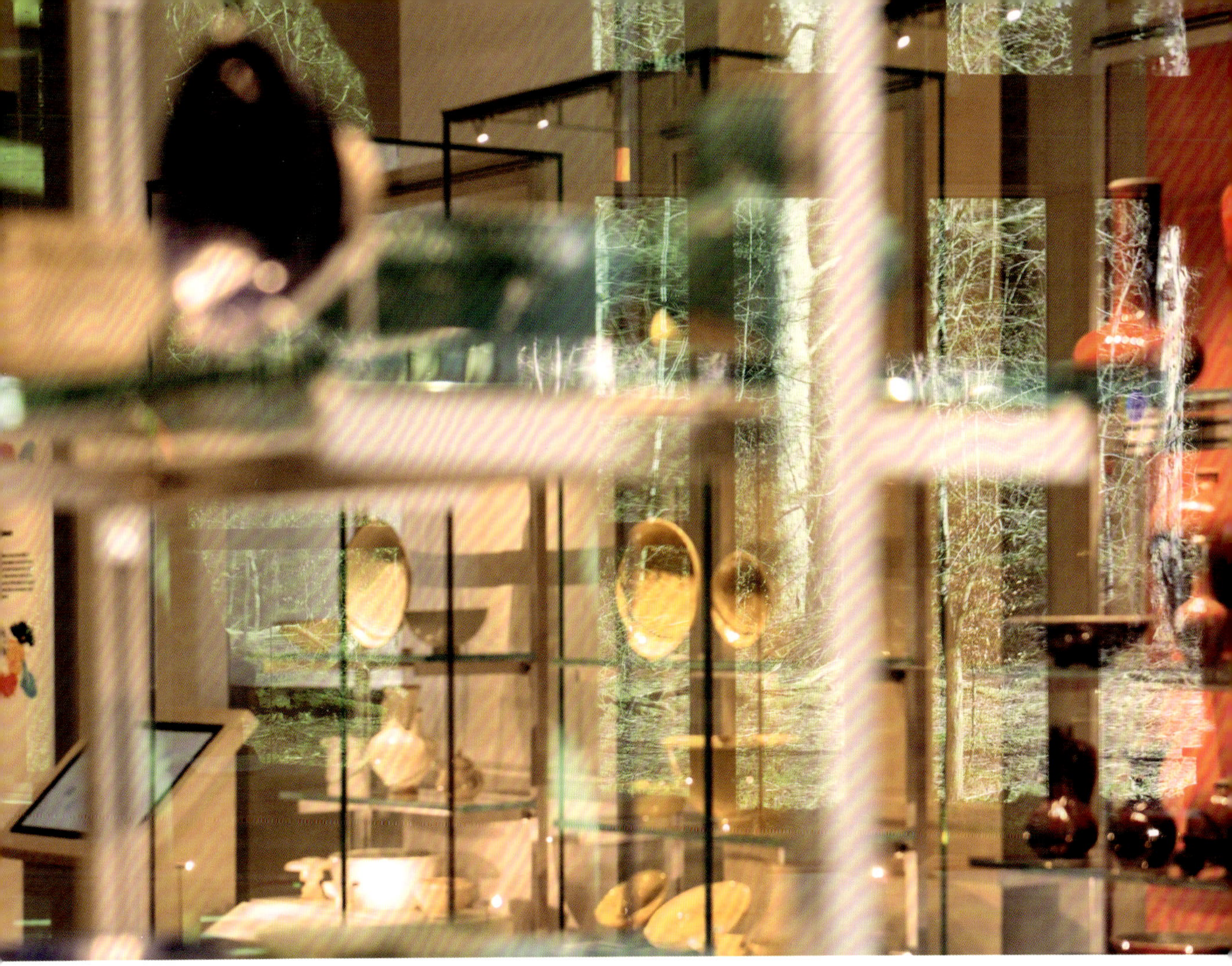

The Pollok Country Park
woodland reflected in the
Colour Gallery object cases.

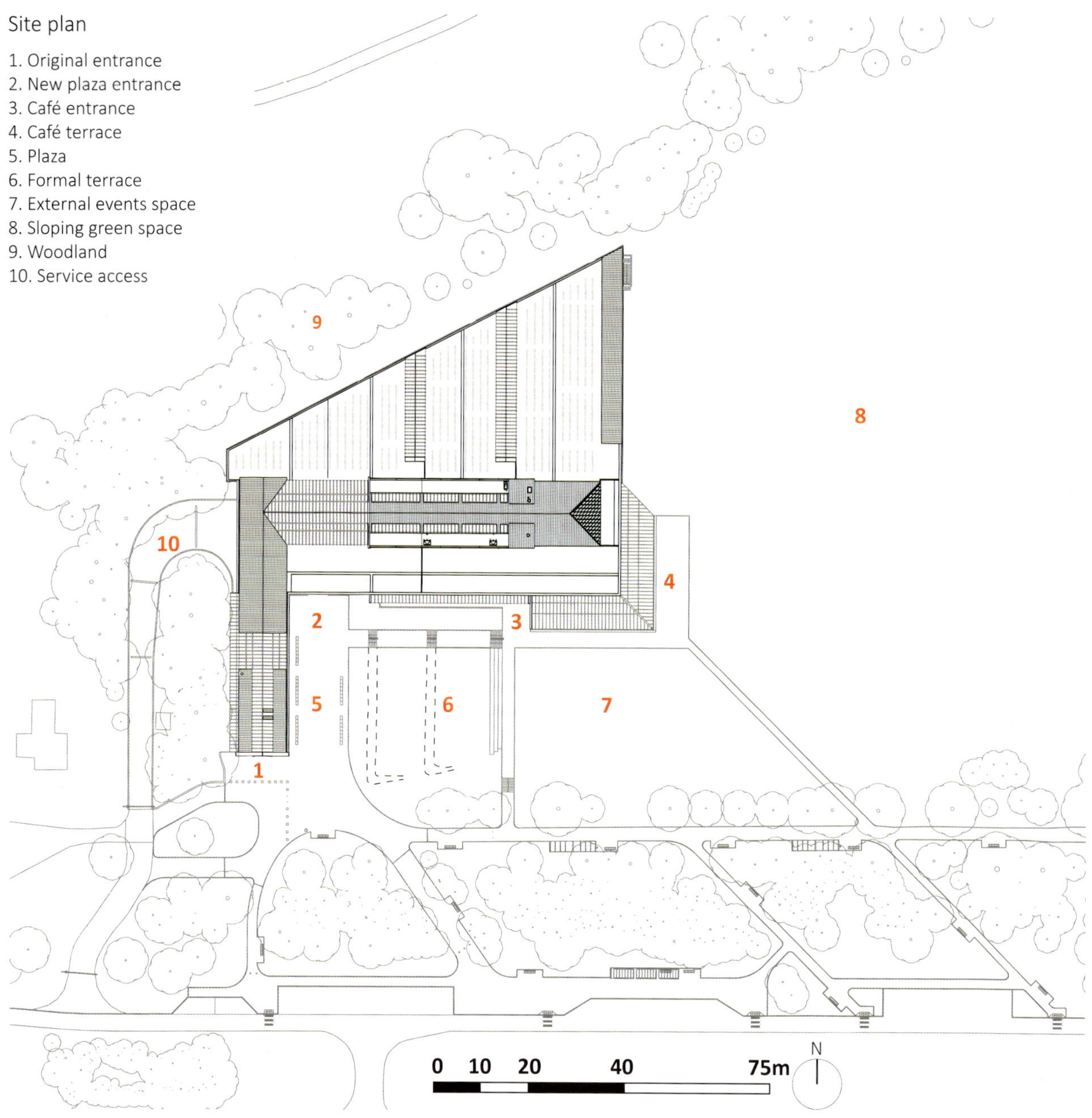

Site plan

1. Original entrance
2. New plaza entrance
3. Café entrance
4. Café terrace
5. Plaza
6. Formal terrace
7. External events space
8. Sloping green space
9. Woodland
10. Service access

9
8
10
4
2
3
1
5
6
7

0   10   20   40   75m

N

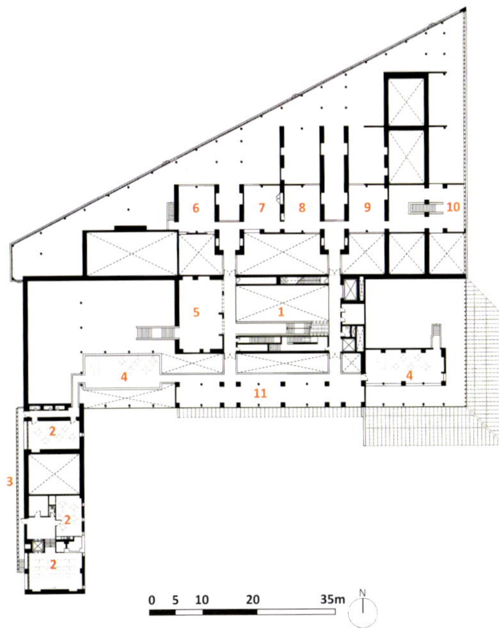

Mezzanine

1. Void above the Central Hub and staircase
2. Learning and Community Wing (former residence)
3. Glazed covered walkway
4. Picnic areas

Makers Galleries
5. Blacksmith and Metalworkers
6. Potters
7. Stonemasons
8. Carvers
9. Artists working on paper
10. Weavers
11. Glaziers and Glassmakers

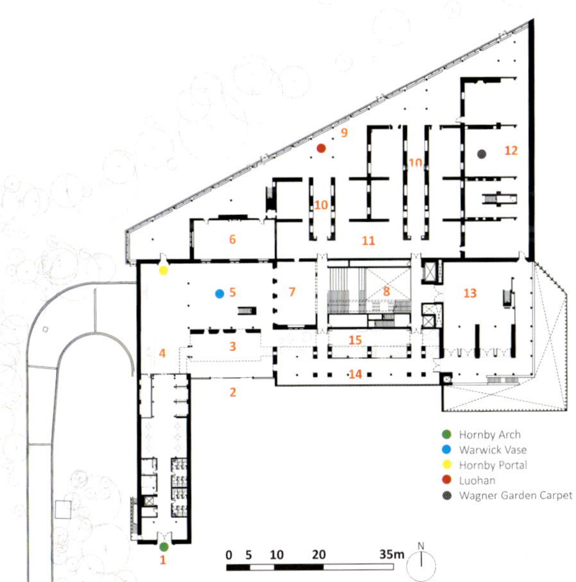

Ground-floor plan

1. Original entrance
2. Plaza entrance
3. Visitor orientation (former Hutton Dining Room)
4. Reception
5. Italian-style courtyard and Warwick Vase
6. Burrells at Home gallery (former Hutton Drawing Room)
7. Burrells in Glasgow gallery (former Burrells' Hall)
8. Central Hub and staircase (former Lecture Theatre)
9. North Gallery 'walk in the woods'
10. North Gallery short / long corridors
11. Central Galleries
12. East Galleries
13. Southeast Storytelling Gallery
14. South Stained-glass Galleries
15. Shop

for security and environmental purposes, and to retain the natural setting with minimal intervention – but potentially also influenced by budget constraints for the landscaping.

New technologies now allow for higher levels of security and environmental control; however, public expectation of better access and inclusivity meant that a new, larger entrance to the collection to suit modern needs was required. The original heritage entrance has been retained alongside this, allowing Gasson's original articulated approach and entrance to the building to still be experienced.

John McAslan + Partners has increased the scale of formal hard landscaping and accessible paths leading to the building to support these two points of access – old and new – and each has then been carefully utilised in the provision of different internal and external facilities. The introduction of a new entrance to the café – previously only accessed from within the building – and the new plaza approach, providing a more expansive public gathering and events space and

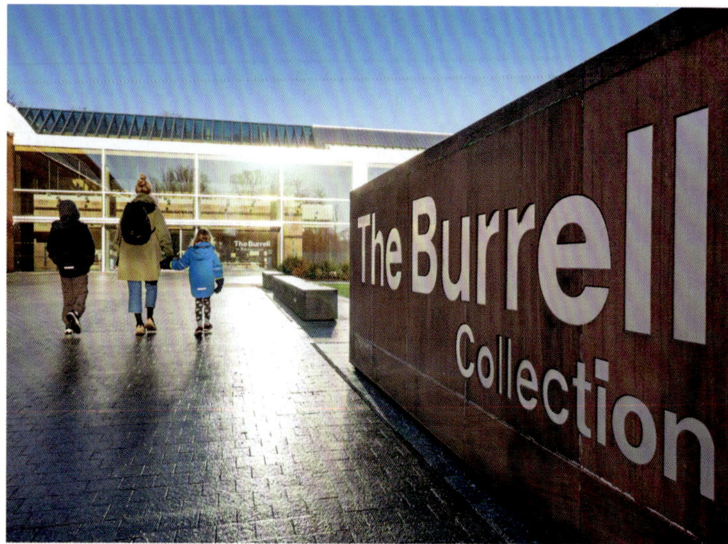

New signage greets visitors on arrival.

echoing the internal Italian-style courtyard, are practical interventions for the arrival of larger visitor groups. Notably sophisticated in their execution, they are sensitive to the original façade and sit comfortably alongside what came before. A new visitor arrival sign has also been introduced, a large pink stone monolith with text relief 'The Burrell Collection', which is physically separated from the building to retain its architectural heritage integrity.

Gasson's original scheme included an accurate reproduction of the Dining Room, Drawing Room and Hall of the Burrells' home, Hutton Castle, each featuring a collection of furniture and interiors dating from between 1200 and 1930. These were considered the most important three rooms within Hutton Castle, and it was William Burrell's express wish in the Memorandum of Agreement of 1944 concerning the gift

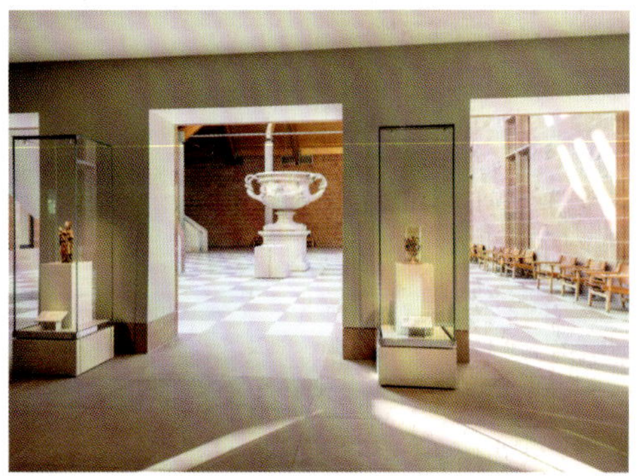

The Burrells in Glasgow gallery looking towards the courtyard.

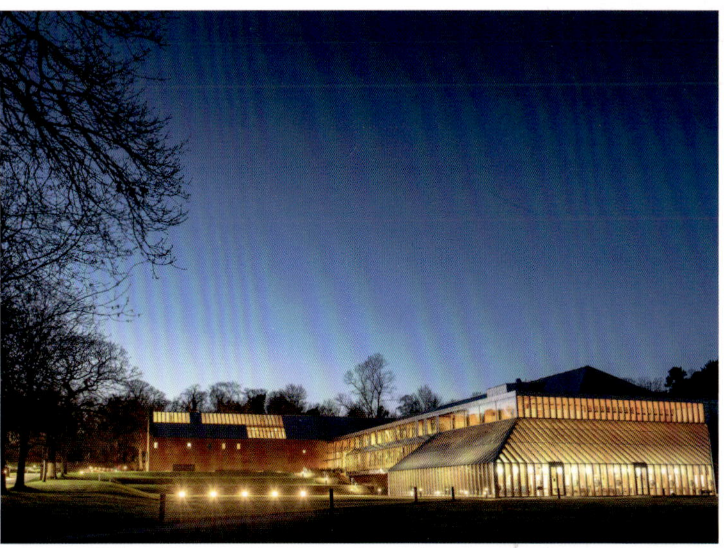

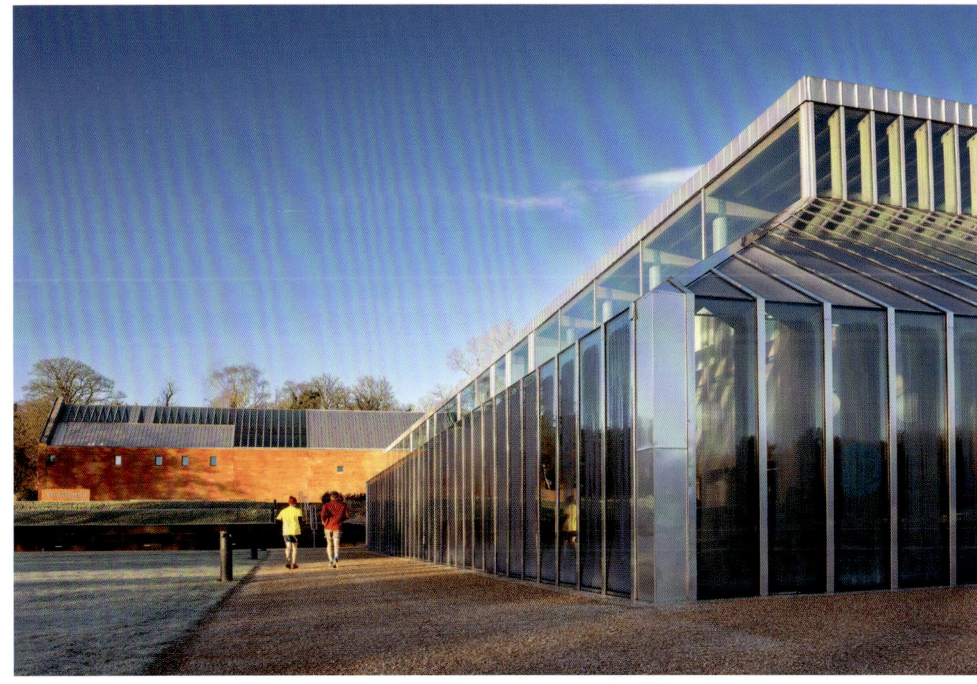

The new café terrace
and entrance.

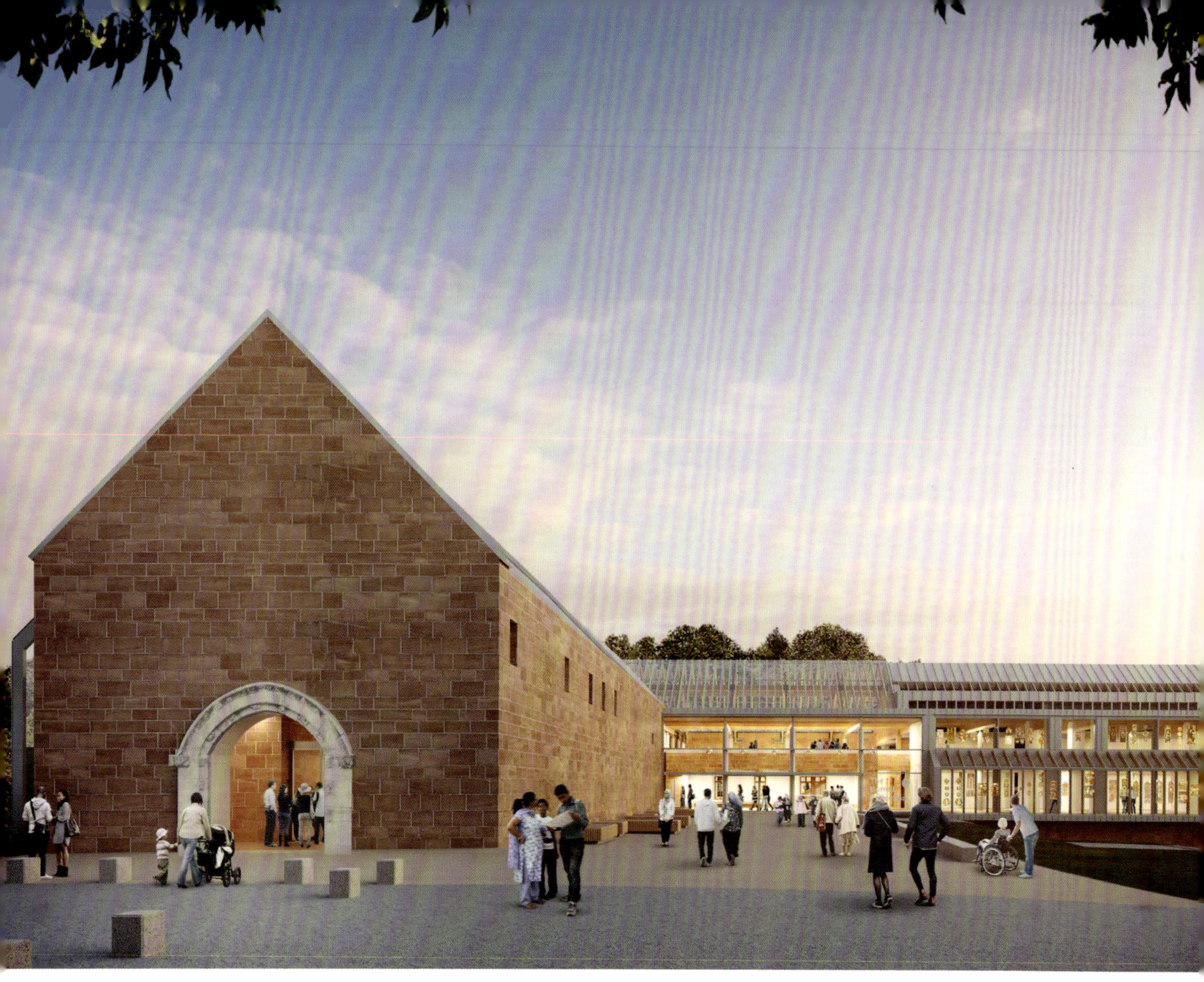

Artist's impression of
the plaza approach to
the entrances.

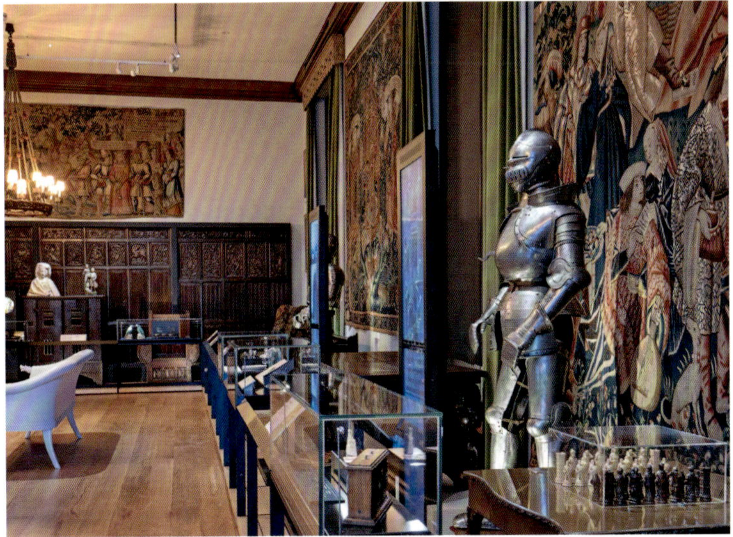

The new Burrells at Home gallery.

at its the centre. Here, the glass canopies continue to flood the space with natural light so that visitors can enjoy the drama of Glasgow's cloud-filled sky – a place to relax and reflect for a few moments before embarking on their museum journey.

Conservation work was all that was needed in the courtyard. However, research indicated that the Hutton Rooms needed to be rethought as their settings were not engaging; visitors had only a restricted view into their interiors from small cordoned-off areas at each doorway, and most only spent a few seconds viewing these galleries. Therefore, in a bold move that sought a modern take on Burrell's desire for his home environment to be documented, the Hutton Rooms were fully reimagined to focus more on the Burrells and their home life rather than replicating the rooms.

of the collection to the city that they should be reproduced in the new museum building. Any changes to them during the refurbishment process were therefore subject to Historic Environment Scotland scrutiny and required approval from the Board of Trustees.

The rooms surrounded Gasson's Italian-style inner courtyard, a large-volume gathering space with the Warwick Vase

The Dining Room to the south was remodelled to create a new visitor orientation leading from the new external plaza. The Burrells' Hall to the east has been reinterpreted to tell the story of the Burrells in Glasgow, and to provide further access routes to John McAslan's new three-level Central Hub at the core of the building, and to the café. And finally, the Drawing Room to the north has undergone a substantial curatorial redisplay telling the story of the Burrells' home life against the setting in which they lived.

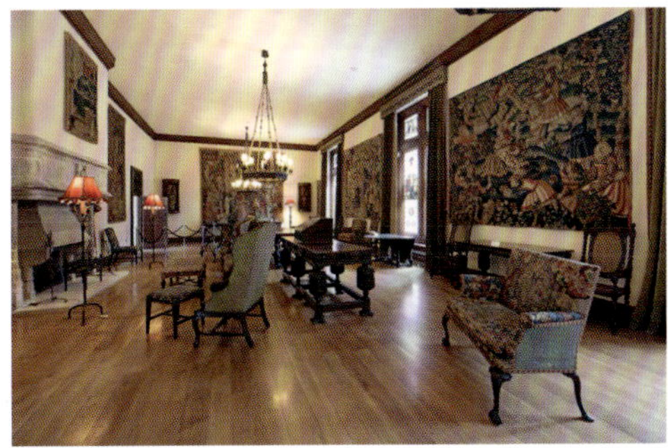

The replica Hutton Drawing Room prior to refurbishment in 2016, now the Burrells at Home gallery.

The North Gallery and Central Galleries

The North Gallery has always been one of the most popular and enchanting spaces within the building. Described by Gasson at the time it was designed as the 'walk in the woods', it is reflective of the walk through the woodland park to get to the museum. This gallery space very much embodies the original design ethos, harmoniously bringing together the synergies of the visitors' journey through the museum, the collection objects and the natural landscape. According to a public vote, the most popular object in the museum is the Luohan, an almost life-size seated Buddhist statue. It was made by artisan Liu Zhen during the Chenghua Reign (1465–87) of the Ming Dynasty (1368–1644) at the imperial kilns in Jingdezhen, southeast China. Perhaps it is not coincidental that this object is displayed so effectively in the North Gallery.

Except for replacement glazing and new service infrastructure, the North Gallery space has not been changed, and its architectural design integrity and charm remain. The introduction of new, modernised display cases, however, given that these were very much 'designed' elements of Gasson's original scheme, required great care as they formed part of the historic listing and character of the building. Gasson's elevation of the natural stone floor to display level (in essence creating a stone plinth) to present each object to the viewer within the backdrop

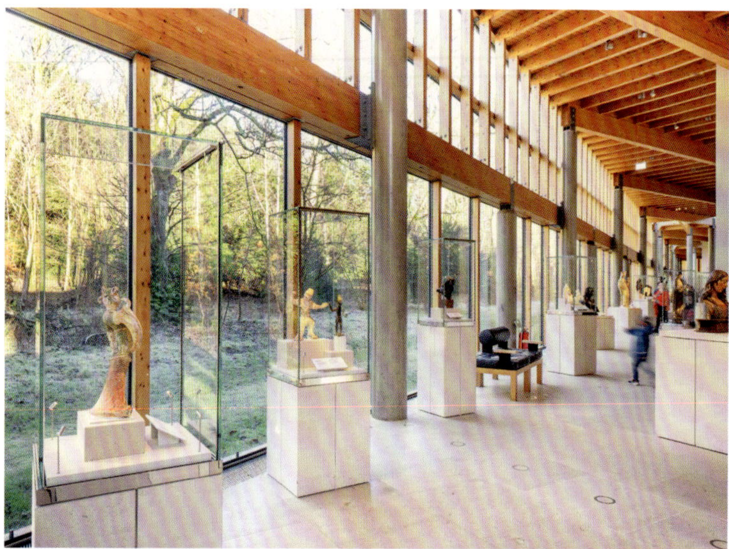

The North Gallery 'walk in the woods'.

of the natural landscape mirrored the objects having been created from natural materials derived from the earth, crafted by the creativity of the human mind and the skill and dexterity of human hands. Introducing new cases into this setting would be extremely challenging.

Contemporary museum cases have far more environmental control and better lighting, along with modern glass that provides superior visual transparency and security. Glasgow Life Museums undertook a large number of investigative studies and prototype testing with various audiences to fully understand the functional and aesthetic requirements for the new cases. The result is a collaboration of high-quality aesthetic and sophisticated product engineering, by museum case experts Maeyvert and museum fit-out specialists Beck, to

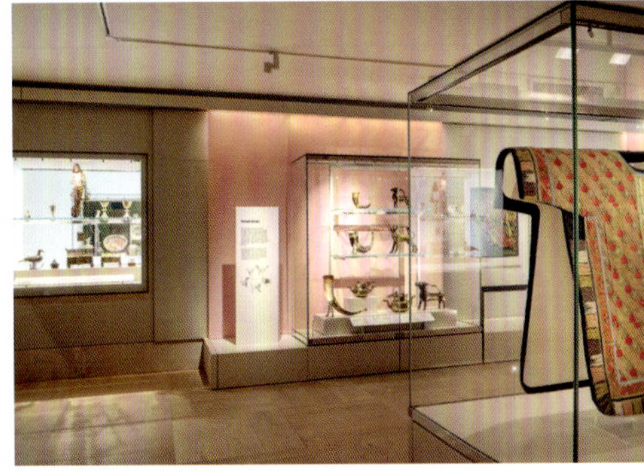

The 15th-century Luohan statue installed in the North Gallery.

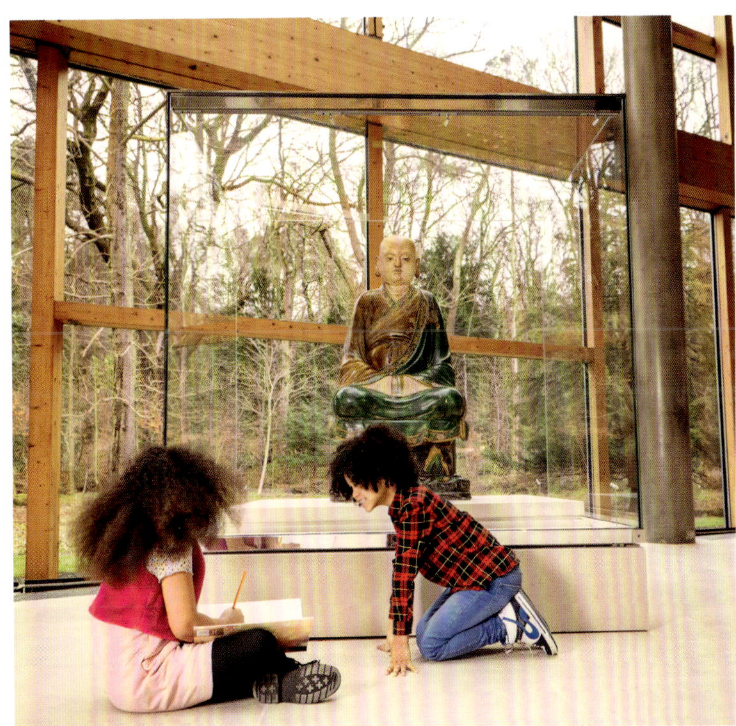

carefully replicate the original design ideology and functional need. The simplicity of the design solution artfully hides the challenges and precision engineering required of a modern museum case whilst retaining the clarity Gasson envisaged. The new display cases are indeed a modern example of human creativity in our technological and digital age, very much in keeping with the ethos of the collection itself.

Minor remodelling changes to the Central Galleries provide better daylight control. The main changes to these galleries are curatorial, providing innovative and engaging interpretation that explores the lives of the objects: What are they? What have they witnessed? What have they experienced? With whom have they come into contact? From where have they come? The Colour Gallery and the Bodies Gallery are notable examples of this multisensory and immersive interpretive approach.

New exhibition cases installed in the Colour Gallery.

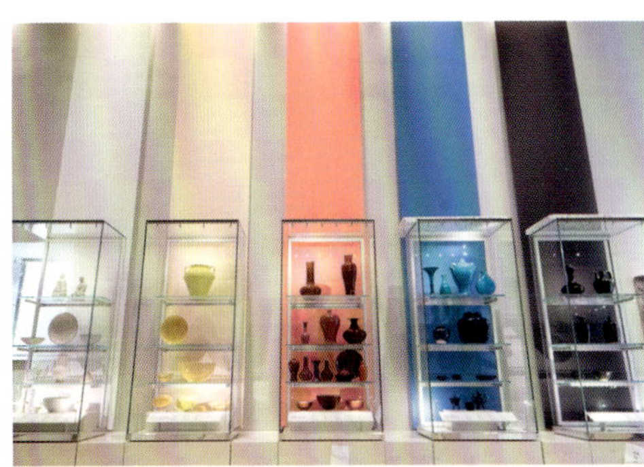

The East Galleries

At the end of the highly immersive North Gallery 'walk in the woods' lie the East Galleries, which display the exceptional and internationally important tapestry collection. However, in the analysis of the original design these galleries were deemed to be too shallow in depth, with limited display space. Visitor surveys revealed that most people did not progress along this route, preferring instead to turn back towards the 'walk in the woods', sadly missing out on the beautiful artefacts held within.

Interestingly, Gasson's early design drawings show various iterations of the southeast corner of the 'walk' and the intended progression to the tapestry display spaces, leading to speculation that there may have been conflicting design priorities at play here. It was an area of the original design that seemed unresolved, and was therefore given much thought during the refurbishment.

Ultimately, the East Galleries have been remodelled to provide a considerable increase in depth and volume, encouraging visitors to explore the tapestries in more detail. This more generous display space also allows comfortable and in-depth viewing of the objects, and the addition of digital screens provides a far richer interpretation of the tapestry collection. A star object in these galleries is the extremely rare seventeenth-century Wagner Garden Carpet, one of the oldest surviving Persian paradise carpets, and a masterpiece of Islamic art.

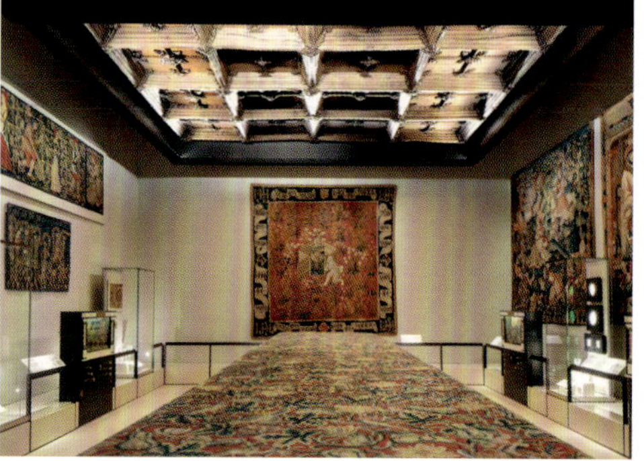

Tapestries and the Bridgwater Ceiling in the East Galleries.

At the end of the East Galleries is the former temporary exhibition space now known as the Southeast Storytelling Gallery, which has been repurposed to provide more double-height space for the effective display of the tapestry collection.

The Southeast Storytelling Gallery.

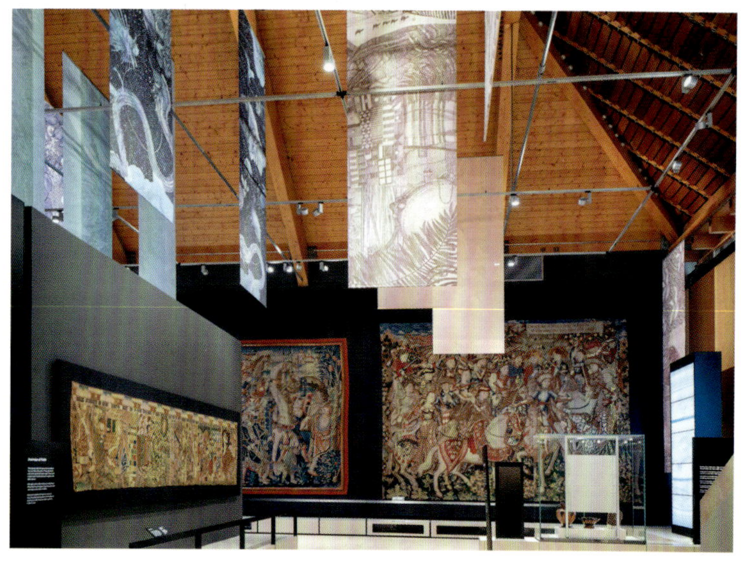

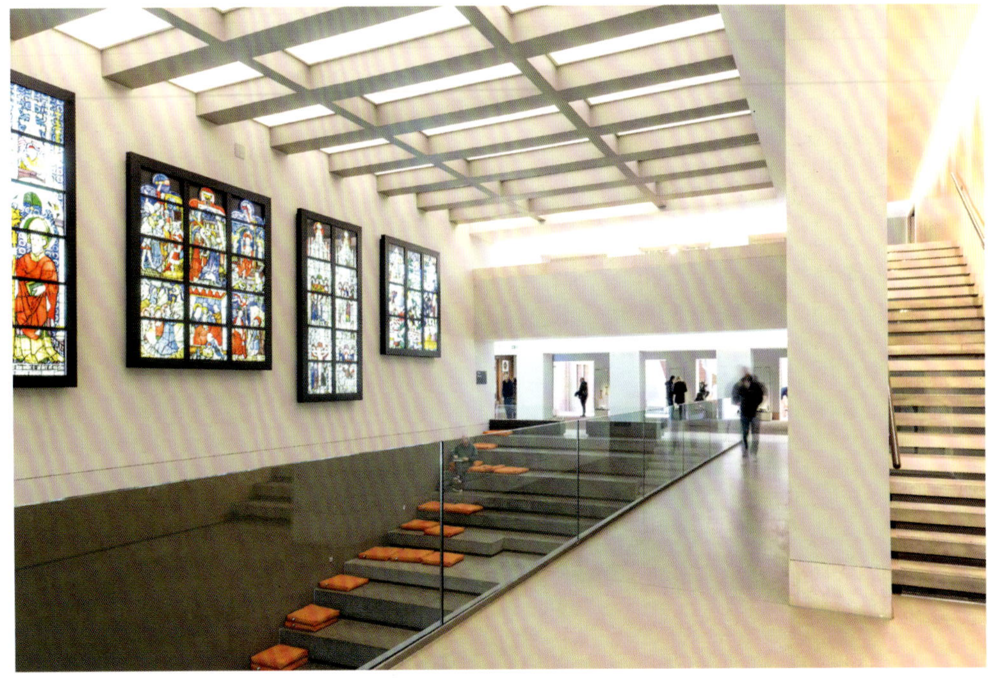

Stained-glass panels displayed within the Central Hub.

The Central Hub and staircase

Whilst the subtle changes made elsewhere should not be overlooked as being highly sophisticated steps in reimagining Gasson's intent for the Burrell Collection, it is the new Central Hub that is McAslan's most significant and immediately apparent intervention, creating a completely redefined volumetric space at the very core of the building – a modern-day agora as envisaged in Event Communications' masterplan. This was previously the location of the largely underused Lecture Theatre, which did not comply with modern accessibility standards, and has been completely removed. It also functioned as the main structural spine of the building and had been constructed of thick reinforced concrete, so its removal

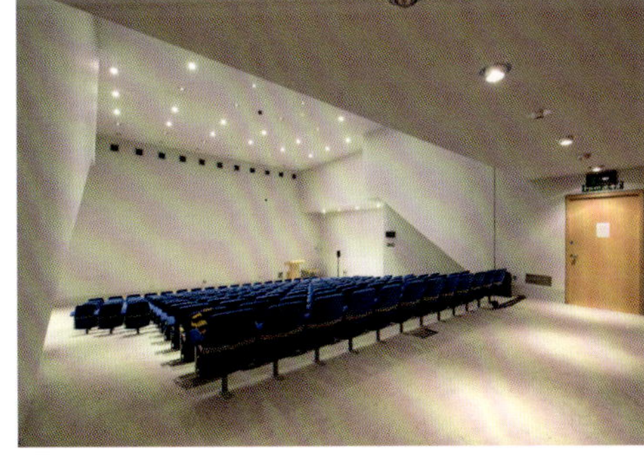

The sloping Lecture Theatre, with podium at the front, prior to the Central Hub and staircase build.

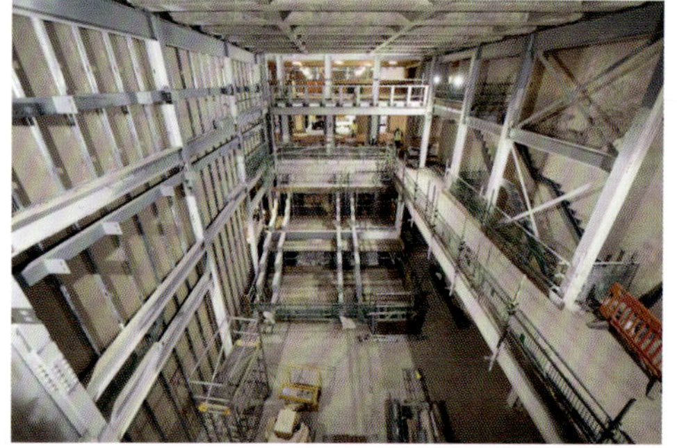

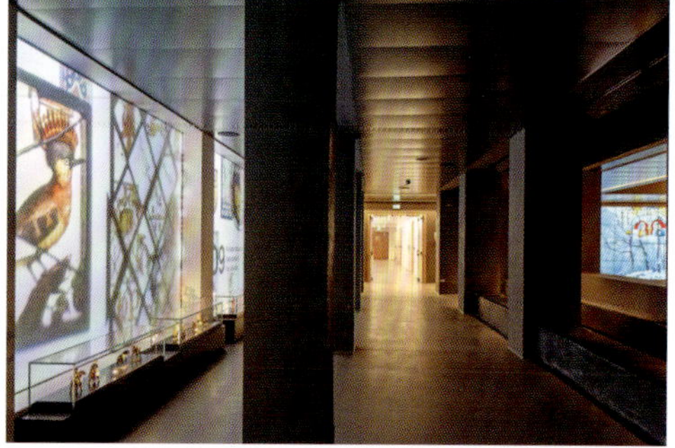

was a considerable undertaking and challenge for the structural engineer David Narro Associates. Demolition involved continual monitoring of structural movement across the rest of the building to ensure structural integrity, not least because some of the collection itself remained *in situ* and formed part of the building fabric.

Construction challenges aside, the resultant Central Hub space is proving to be a great intervention, providing a calm and contemplative circulation point at the centre of the museum that invites visitors to pause, take a seat – the staircase has a dual purpose, providing seating and a means of connecting two floors – and absorb what they have seen. In addition, it not only provides improved horizontal and vertical connectivity and orientation, but also highlights the further opening up of the building to the public, with new galleries on the mezzanine floor and connection to the Collection Stores on the lower-ground floor.

The Collection Stores

Guided tours of the stores – where objects not on display are stored – from the bottom of the Central Hub staircase now give a fascinating and much deeper insight into the collection. This curatorial change means the sheer scale and diversity of what is held at the museum is more apparent and accessible. Integral to this 'opening up', the large digital displays and seating areas within the new Central Hub form an internal public amphitheatre – somewhat reminiscent of the former Lecture Theatre – which visually and physically connects to the lower-level stores.

The mezzanine and upper levels

Connected to the Central Hub by both a lift and new central staircases, the mezzanine level has new galleries that occupy the former office and administrative spaces, providing additional linear space to display the substantial stained-glass collection.

The glass art is now displayed in front of the glass façade that runs along this edge of the building and can be viewed in natural light, as originally intended. From the outside, the glass animates this view with a rich graphic tapestry of texture and colour – quite a remarkable sight when viewed from outside in the early evening, illuminated by the interior light of the building itself.

The other existing galleries on this level, known as the Makers Galleries, look

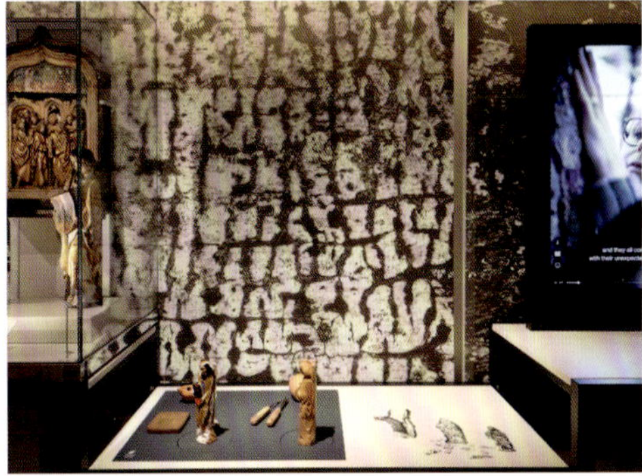

at how objects are made. They have undergone a complete redisplay with new digital and tactile interpretation methods that tell the story of the lives of the objects before they came to be part of the Burrell Collection.

Staff and administration offices, and a community meeting room, occupy the upper floor. Conservation studios were formerly sited here, but the museum conservation activities have now been relocated to new, purpose-built spaces at the nearby Glasgow Museums Resource Centre.

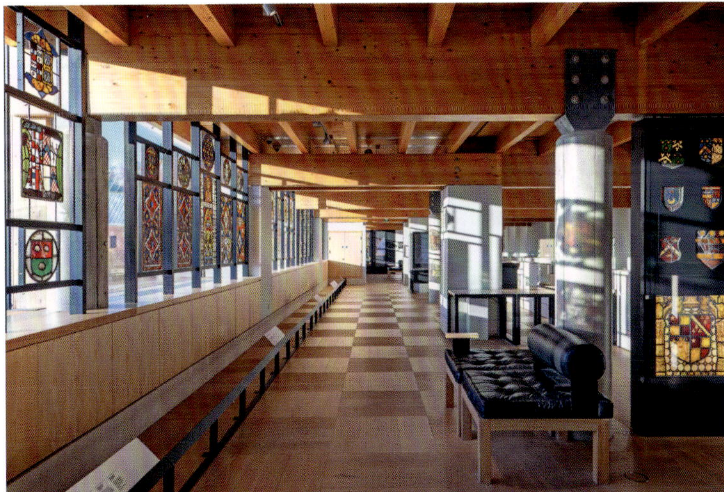

The Stained-Glass Galleries on the mezzanine level.

Improved visitor experience and facilities

Creative design interventions, and an improved café and retail offering; have markedly enhanced the visitor experience. New ancillary facilities including additional accessible toilets, two Changing Places toilets that provide extra space and hoists, family areas and amenities for school groups, along with quiet rooms for groups with additional needs all provide a far more inclusive environment. A notable contribution to greater economic and social inclusion is the three new picnic areas where visitors can enjoy their own food and drink. What is notable is that these are not small or hidden-away spaces within the building, but mostly occupy prominent areas of high visual value.

The new Learning and Community Wing occupies the former visiting academic residence – a two-bedroom flat on the upper floor – which sits next to what is now the Makers Stained-Glass Gallery. Whilst remodelling of this area has been minimal, there has been a significant shift in function; it is now a high-quality public space for further exploration of the collection through art and crafts classes. The roof lights in the double-height space provide natural light, and windows visually connect the occupants to the surrounding natural landscape. The external glazed covered walkway that was formerly the private entrance to the residence – and a direct link to the landscape – has been reutilised to provide public access to the new wing.

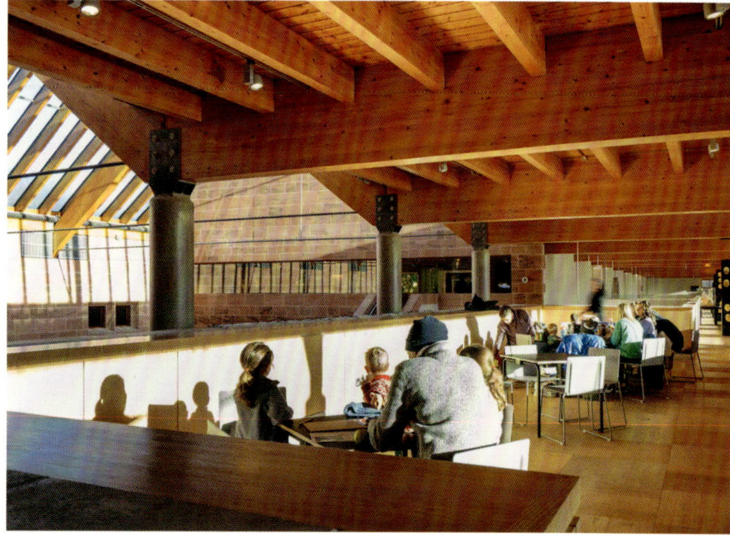

One of the new picnic areas being enjoyed by visitors.

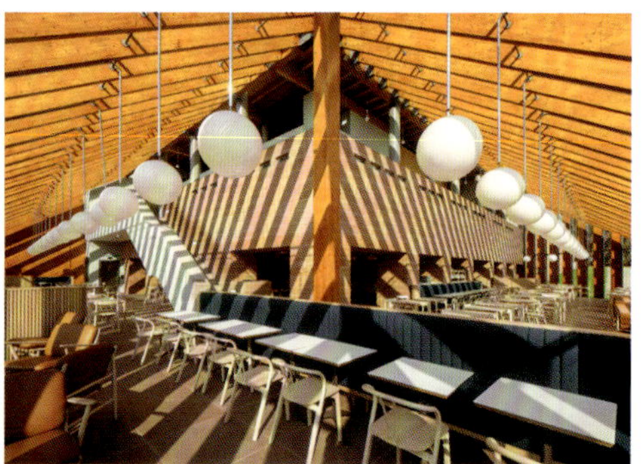

Sun streams through the vertical wooden beams in the restaurant.

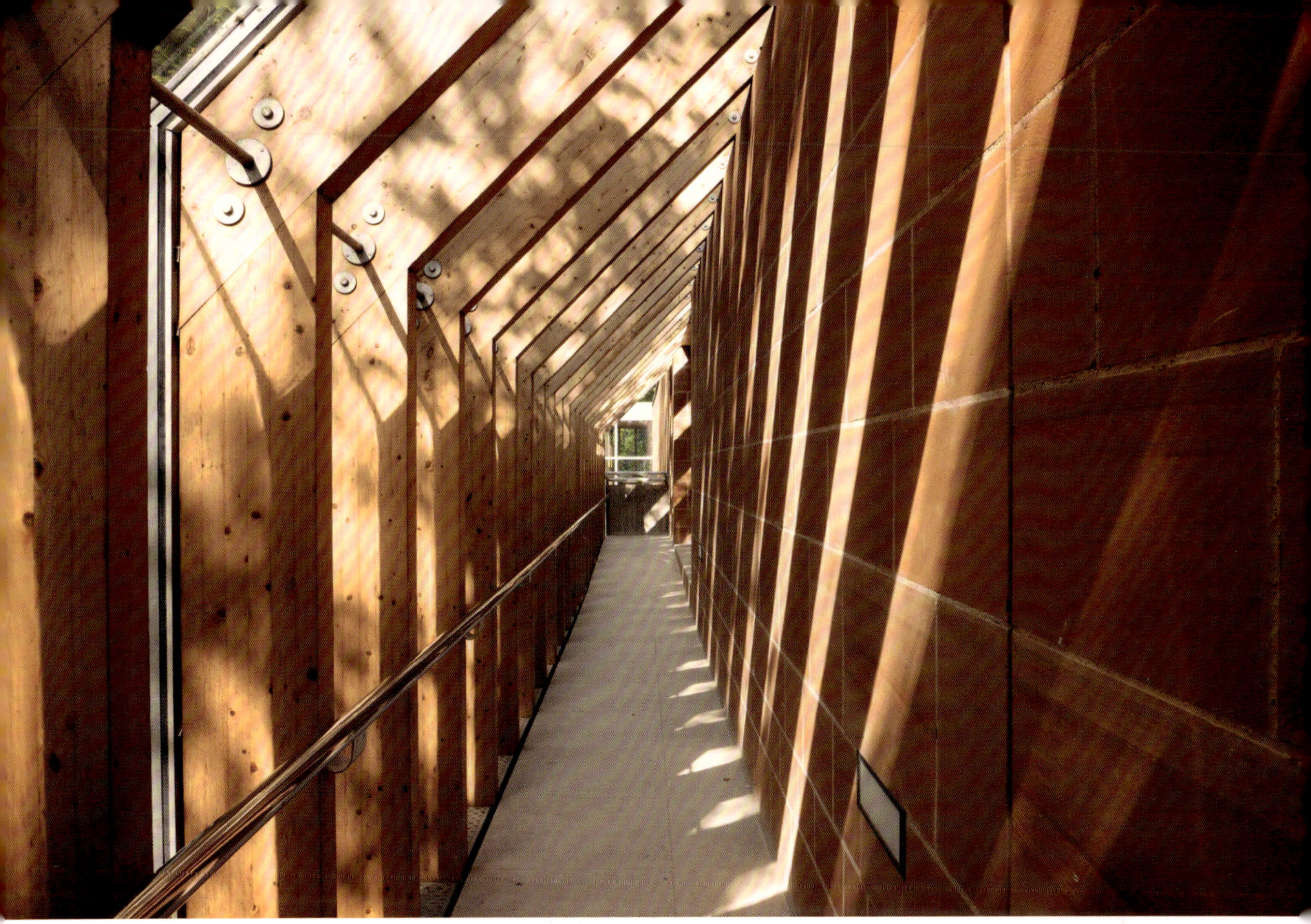

Walkway to the Learning and Community Wing.

A fully accessible Changing Places toilet.

A room in the annexed Learning and Community Wing.

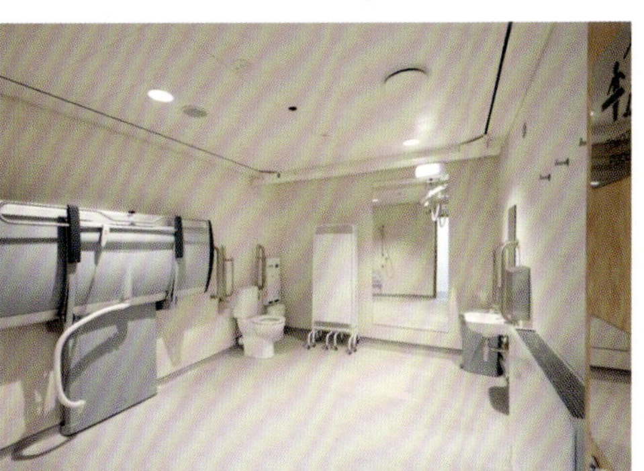

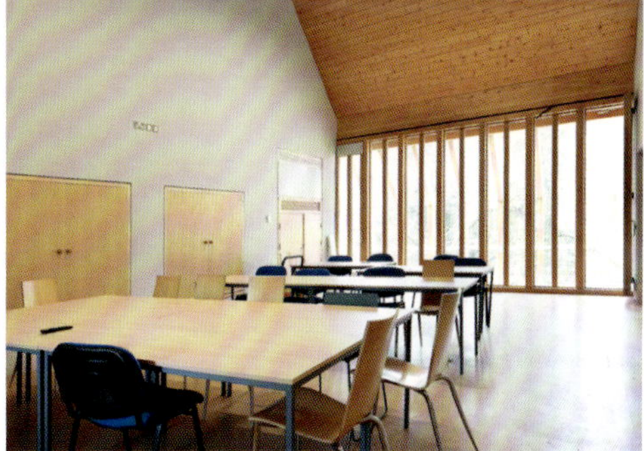

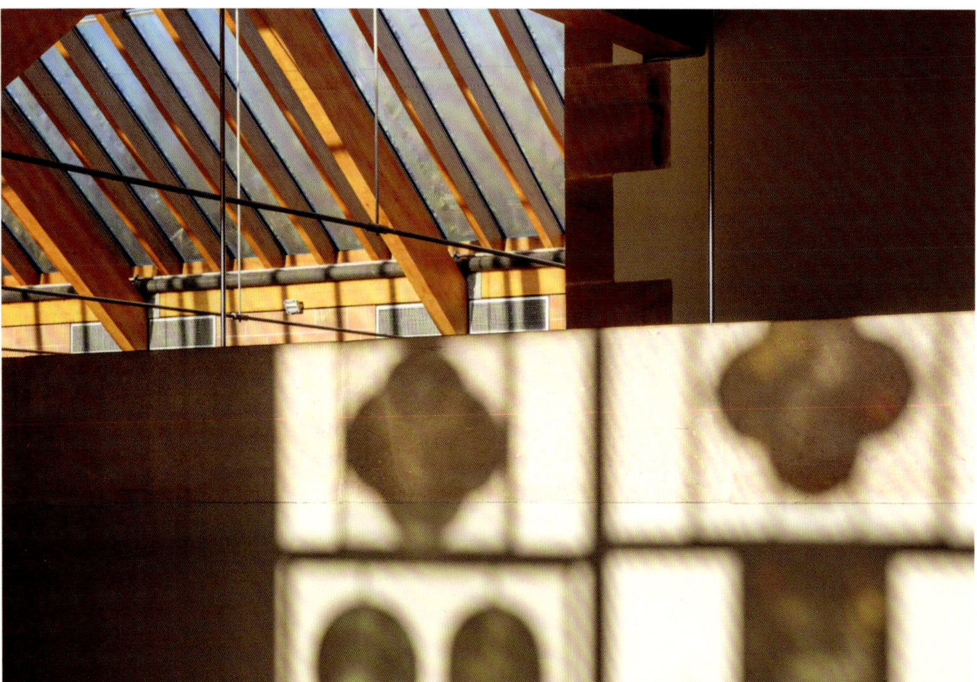

Stone, wood, glass and metal are used throughout the Burrell Collection building.

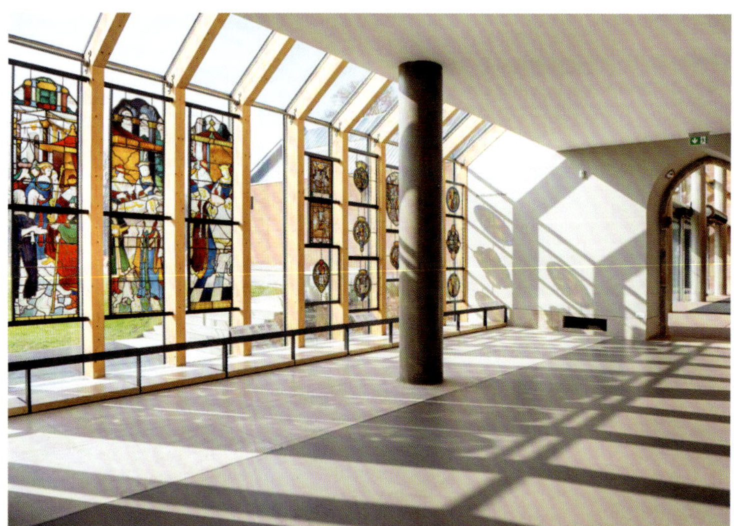

Polished concrete floors have replaced formerly carpeted areas.

Materiality and colour

As conceived by Gasson, so that the objects remained the focus of the spaces, the original building utilises a limited palette of materials and colours, symbolising the natural environment. Stone and wood represent the earth and the qualities of the landscape itself, whilst glass and metal were utilised to reflect the sky.

McAslan's material interventions were generally focused on conservation and restoration. Where additional architectural elements have been introduced, such as the Central Hub, new materials have been purposefully utilised to distinguish them from original elements. Typically, a micro-cement finish has been applied to the walls and polished concrete has been used for floors in these new areas. Each was considered to complement the original palette without overshadowing it.

The original stone of the building was sourced locally, from the Locharbriggs Quarry in Dumfries. Unfortunately, the quarry closed some years prior to the renovation, so to maintain the historical integrity and character of the building fabric it was necessary to ask for it to be reopened to mine for a suitable petrographic match. This ensured that the new stone forming the restoration and remodelling works was indistinguishable from the original – a move central to maintaining Gasson's vision. The stone forming the base of the new North Gallery display cases has also been accurately matched to the flooring already *in situ*, and again the historic integrity and aesthetic have not been compromised.

Elsewhere, carpet – also sourced locally, this time from the Isle of Bute – had formerly been used in some of the circulation areas, and despite being of high quality was very much showing its age and in need of replacement. However, given that fabric is no longer considered a suitable material finish for museum settings for reasons of pest control, it has now been replaced with polished concrete, colour-matched to the original carpet.

The main intent of Gasson's original limited palette was to provide a neutral backdrop to the collection to highlight the objects' colours, textures and materials. However, visitor feedback identified that this was not always working as well as it could, making orientation within so large a collection challenging, and effectively taking something critical away from the artefacts. To improve visitor experience and assist with orientation, a limited number of block colours have been introduced to some of the galleries to anchor key spaces within the building. This has been carefully considered in terms of both palette and lighting, with the overall aim of enabling the displays to remain centre stage.

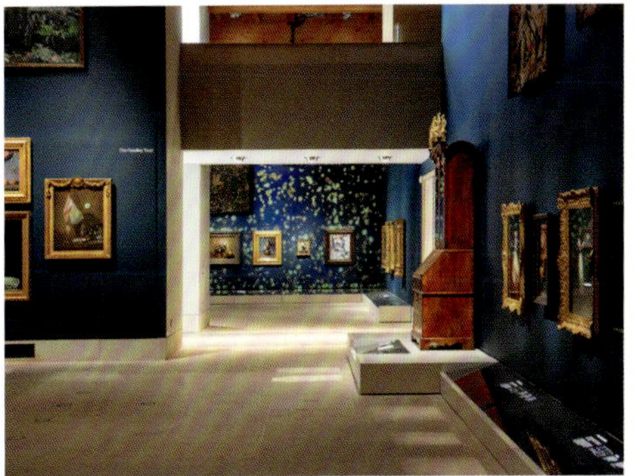

Bold colours aid visitor orientation within internal galleries.

GALLERY DESIGN AND INTERPRETATION

n the years prior to the redevelopment project, Glasgow Life Museums' curatorial team in partnership with several universities and scholars extensively researched the objects, the meaning and significance of the collection, the character and influence of William and Constance Burrell, and the nature of the building. One outcome was the publication of a scholarly catalogue of the tapestry collection in 2017,[18] which had long been an ambition of William Burrell himself. In addition, Glasgow Life Museums' consultation programme and engagement with potential audiences and the local community created a clear vision of who the visitors would be and how they would engage effectively with the new displays. The knowledge was shared with Event Communications who used it to develop, in partnership with the Museums Service, the new masterplan for the Burrell Collection.

Event Communications recognised the importance of understanding the Burrells and their collection, as well as Gasson's architectural philosophy and the symbiotic

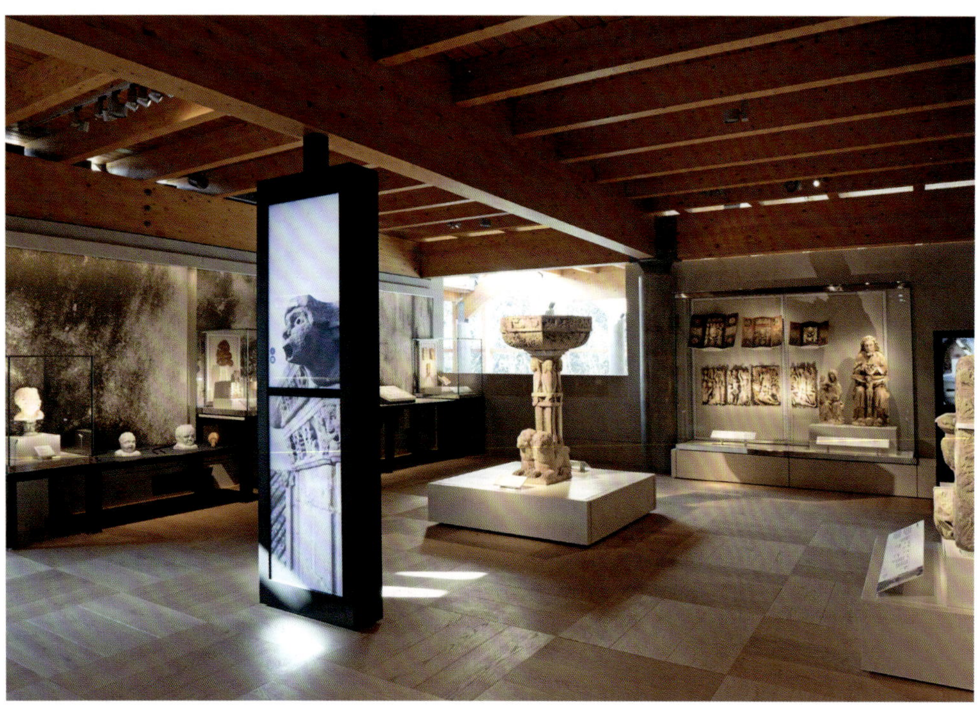

The story-display approach in the Stonemason Makers Gallery.

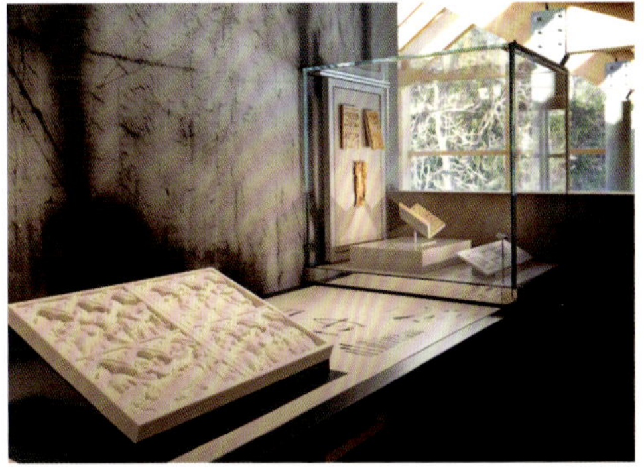

relationship between the objects and the building. In their Concept Design report, they noted:

We believe that any new proposals must be founded on a deep understanding of the original design principles – in effect, that the design team must become fluent in Gasson, Meunier and Andresen's design language before seeking to create new interventions. We have also spent considerable time analysing Sir William Burrell's approach to collecting and the principles that informed his selections, as well as parsing his will to ensure that respect for Sir William's legacy is woven into our thinking. Becoming an inspirational, world class museum means that the Burrell Collection must not only address its immediate problems, it must also bring new meaning to the collecting and design principles embedded within it.[19]

A simple but intelligent proposition was therefore developed that builds on

Glasgow Life Museums' long-established story-display approach, organised over the three floor levels:

Level 1: Collect *See the extraordinary extent and breadth of the collection in the object stores. Explore the coming together of the collection and learn about how it is researched and cared for.*

Level 2: Witness *See from the objects' perspectives. Where have they been? What have they seen? Encounter the people, the places, and activities that the objects have witnessed. Explore the lives of the objects before they came to the Burrell Collection.*

Level 3: Make *Explore the objects through the eyes of the craftspeople, makers and artists who created them. Experience the materials, process, techniques and skills that the objects represent. Explore the lives of the makers – their inspiration and the context in which they worked.*[20]

Within this conceptual framework, the curators developed 221 individual story displays that explore different aspects of the collection in innovative new ways.

Tactile interpretation also now provides physical access to materials, textures and details through touch, successfully bringing the objects out of their cases and into the hands of the visitors, which is so important when sight may not be someone's primary method of engagement with the world.

Digital media

Not previously used within the museum, digital media has now been thoughtfully integrated and provides a richer and more immersive experience of the collection, giving visitors the opportunity to explore the history of, and learn about the objects, their materials and makers by taking them back in time to their creation. The digital display for the Wagner Garden Carpet is an exemplar of how the new technology is used to further enhance the interpretation of the collection. The scaled-up digital landscape provides a better understanding of the three-dimensional characteristics of the beautiful Persian paradise garden it features.

Responding to the ethos of both Burrell and Gasson, the parkland setting of the collection is also now digitally referenced within the Central Hub, actively encouraging wider exploration of the park's ecosystem.

Digital screens aid exploration of the Wagner Garden Carpet.

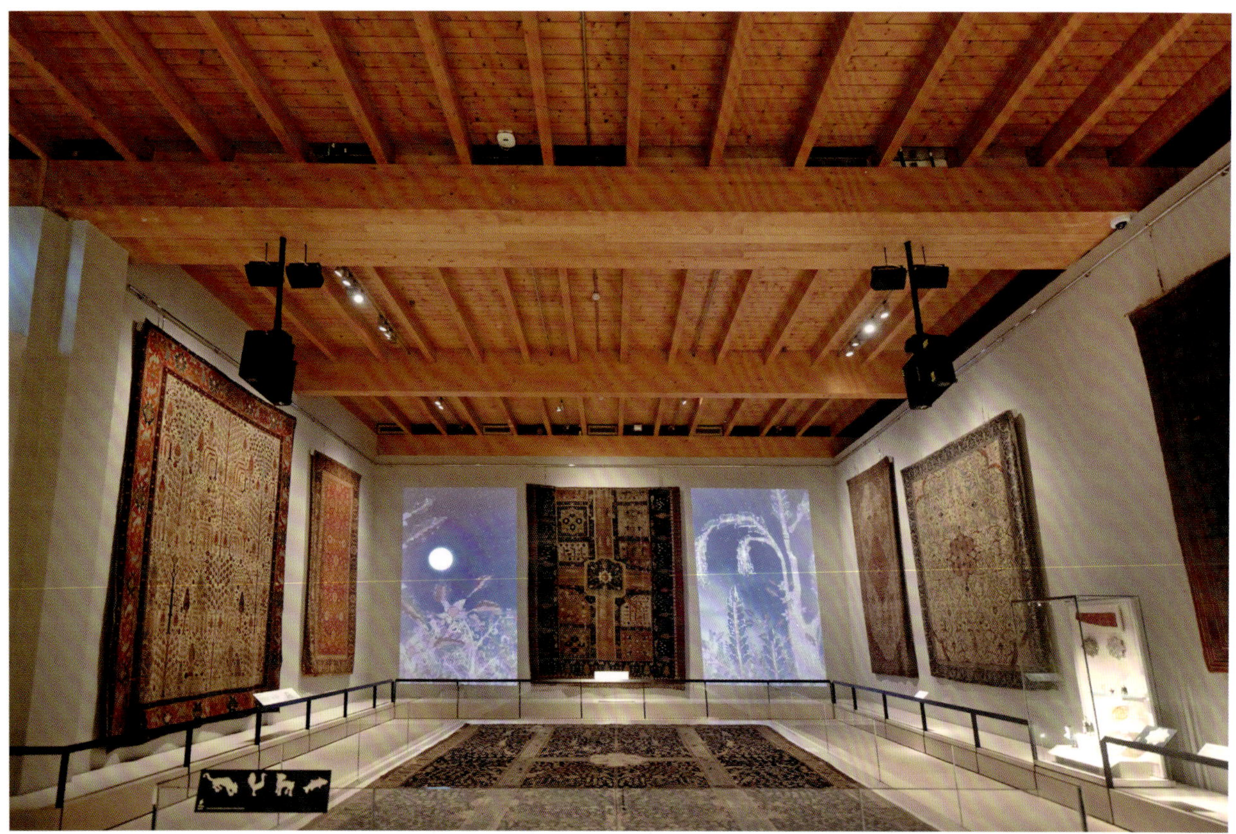

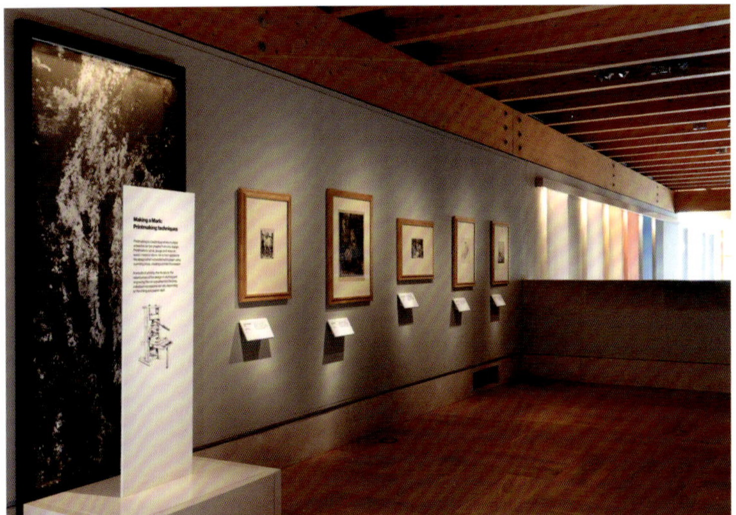

Bespoke lighting solutions in the galleries for light-sensitive collections.

stories. This also reflects Burrell's ambition that the collection be presented as it might naturally be lived with.

McAslan's and Event Communications' solutions are no less bespoke than Gasson's, though the techniques employed are rather different. Sophisticated digital software was used to analyse the effects of natural and artificial light on the objects, then to find the correct technical glazing specification and display lighting for each instance. Their approach enabled curatorial flexibility without compromising Gasson's original visual connections to the external landscape.

Lighting

Several of the design challenges for John McAslan + Partners and Event Communications were similar to those faced by Gasson, most notably dealing with the control of natural light and its impact on the conservation of the objects. Gasson's museum design generally displayed artefacts by material or object grouping, for example tapestries, ceramics and paintings. Light-controlled galleries were designed accordingly, with less light-sensitive displays closest to the glazed perimeter of the building, and more light-sensitive objects kept to the central galleries, deeper into the building plan. However, modern curatorial approaches often require that objects of varying materials and light sensitivities are displayed together to enable the telling of more holistic and engaging

THE CONSTRUCTION WORKS

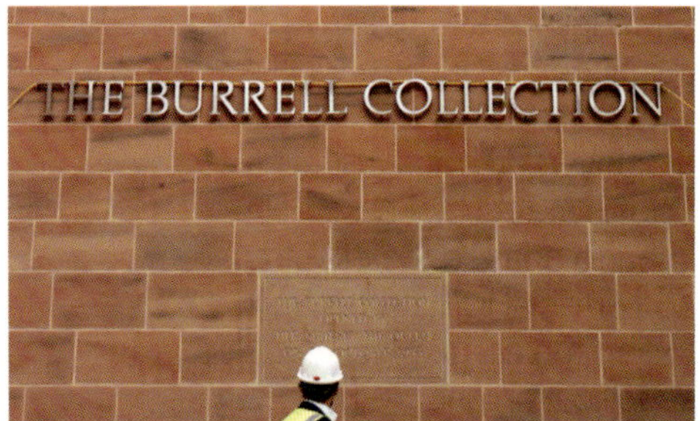

The construction works commenced in 2017 following the decanting of most of the collection artefacts to Glasgow Museums Resource Centre on the south side of the city. However, following risk assessments it became evident that certain architectural objects – mainly those that were integrated into the fabric of the building – would need to remain *in situ* during the construction phase.

In the 1950s, Burrell had made some important acquisitions specifically for the building that would house his collection, and after his death the Burrell Trustees also purchased objects for the same purpose. Indeed, the original architectural brief specified that these collection objects should be considered as part of the building design. Gasson cleverly incorporated these, for example as doors, architraves, ceilings and wall panels, to define and frame important thresholds and vistas along the visitor journey.

Integrating historical architectural objects into the fabric of a modular, modern construction is in itself rare and technically challenging, but for the Burrell Collection, in addition to serving their original functions, they were also required to work as active components within the 'new' public building. Just as this had tested Gasson's original team, so it continued to present the new team with challenges during the restoration.

A protective enclosure was required to prevent physical damage and provide stable environmental conditions to maintain the integrity of the objects whilst the conditions around them were in flux. Conditions were continually monitored throughout the works both on site and remotely from Glasgow Museums Resource Centre. However, demonstrating design functionality of the enclosure and compliance with current standards in

A contractor walking past the original Burrell Collection sign marking the opening of the building by Queen Elizabeth II.

Protective measures were taken to secure the Hornby Portal during the building's refurbishment.

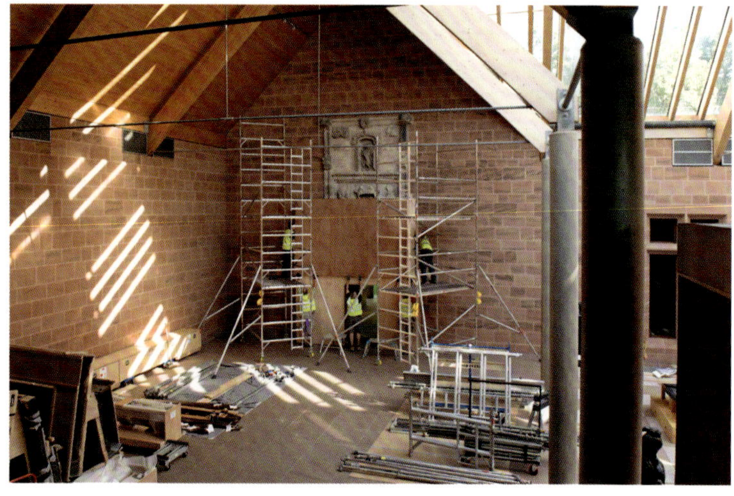

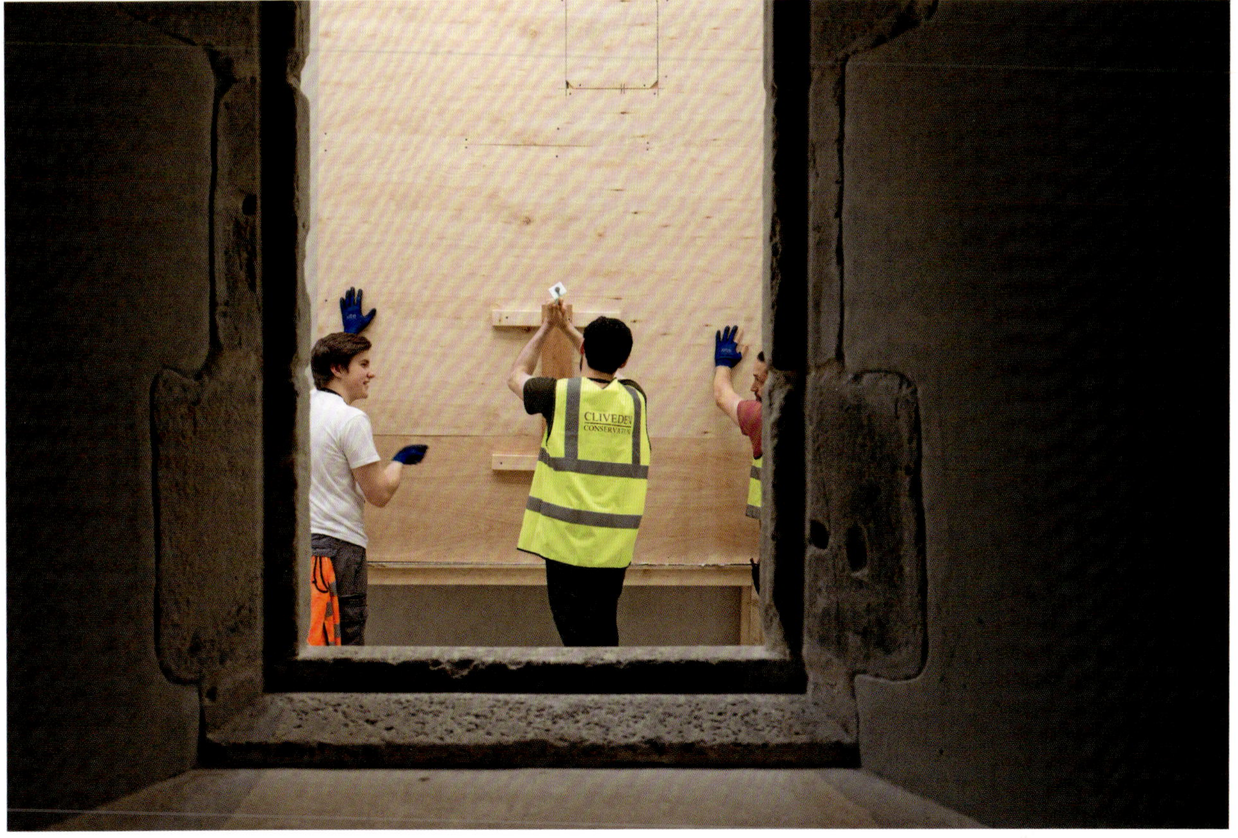

The Italian windows in the North Gallery corridor having their protective enclosures installed before construction began.

building regulations was complicated by a number of factors, one of which was that no British or European certification exists for the fire-resistance rating of, for example, a medieval door. Performance characteristics therefore had to be established through consultation with the curatorial and conservation teams, assessing historical records – and in some instances carrying out investigative conservatorial work – to select the construction materials and methods, and to prove that modern building standards could indeed be met by medieval construction.

Another challenge was the removal of the former Lecture Theatre to create the new Central Hub, a structurally significant undertaking as its walls formed the main structural spine of the building. The initial work involved 24 weeks of careful dismantling of the thick reinforced-concrete theatre, which required continual monitoring of any effects on the remaining

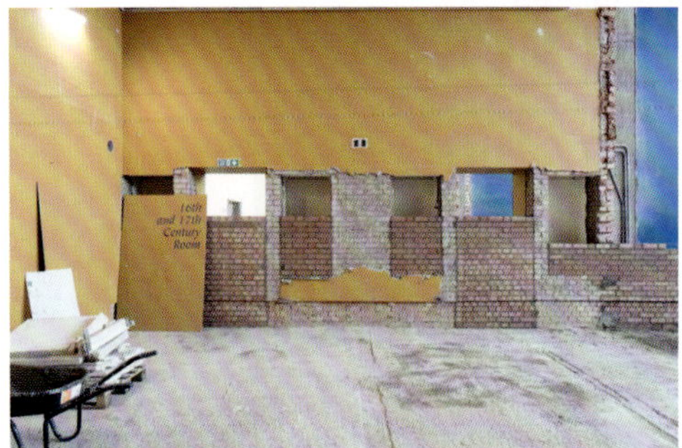

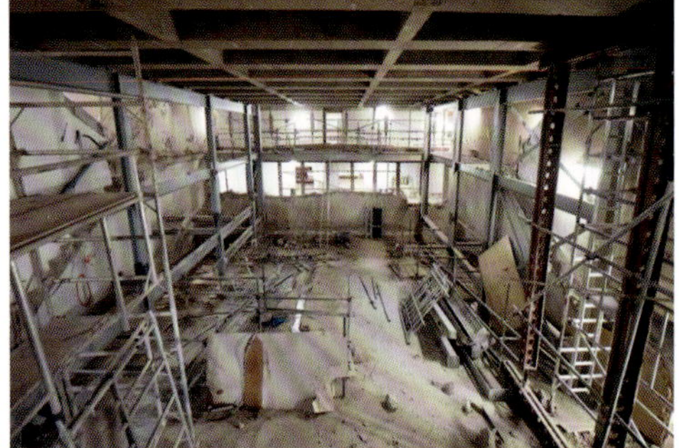

Planning for the unexpected

In March 2020, at the start of the Covid-19 pandemic, the UK and Scottish governments introduced a nationwide 'lockdown' ordering people other than essential workers to stay at home. As a 'Project of National Importance', site work on the Burrell Collection refurbishment was able to resume after the first lockdown ended and the rules were relaxed within the construction industry. However, efficiently progressing the works was in practice very challenging due to the social-distancing rules remaining in place. The risk of a localised outbreak of Covid-19 on site not only posed a health risk for those involved but could have potentially delayed or stopped the construction process entirely. Various site mitigation measures were introduced, such as protective face masks, hand-cleansing stations and self-isolation for site personnel with Covid-like symptoms. But the impact extended far beyond site safety – interruption to global supply chains exacerbated construction challenges and placed uncontrollable strains on timescales, with delivery of specialist services, plant and building components from abroad often delayed or unavailable for long periods.

structure and on the priceless collection objects that remained *in situ*. The same levels of care and observation were required during the remodelling of the East Galleries, also in close proximity to the integrated collection objects, where demolition work had to be undertaken manually, brick by brick, prior to the equally diligent introduction of new structural elements.

Top: Walls were disassembled brick by brick to remodel the East Galleries spaces.

Bottom: Dismantling the Lecture Theatre to create the Central Hub.

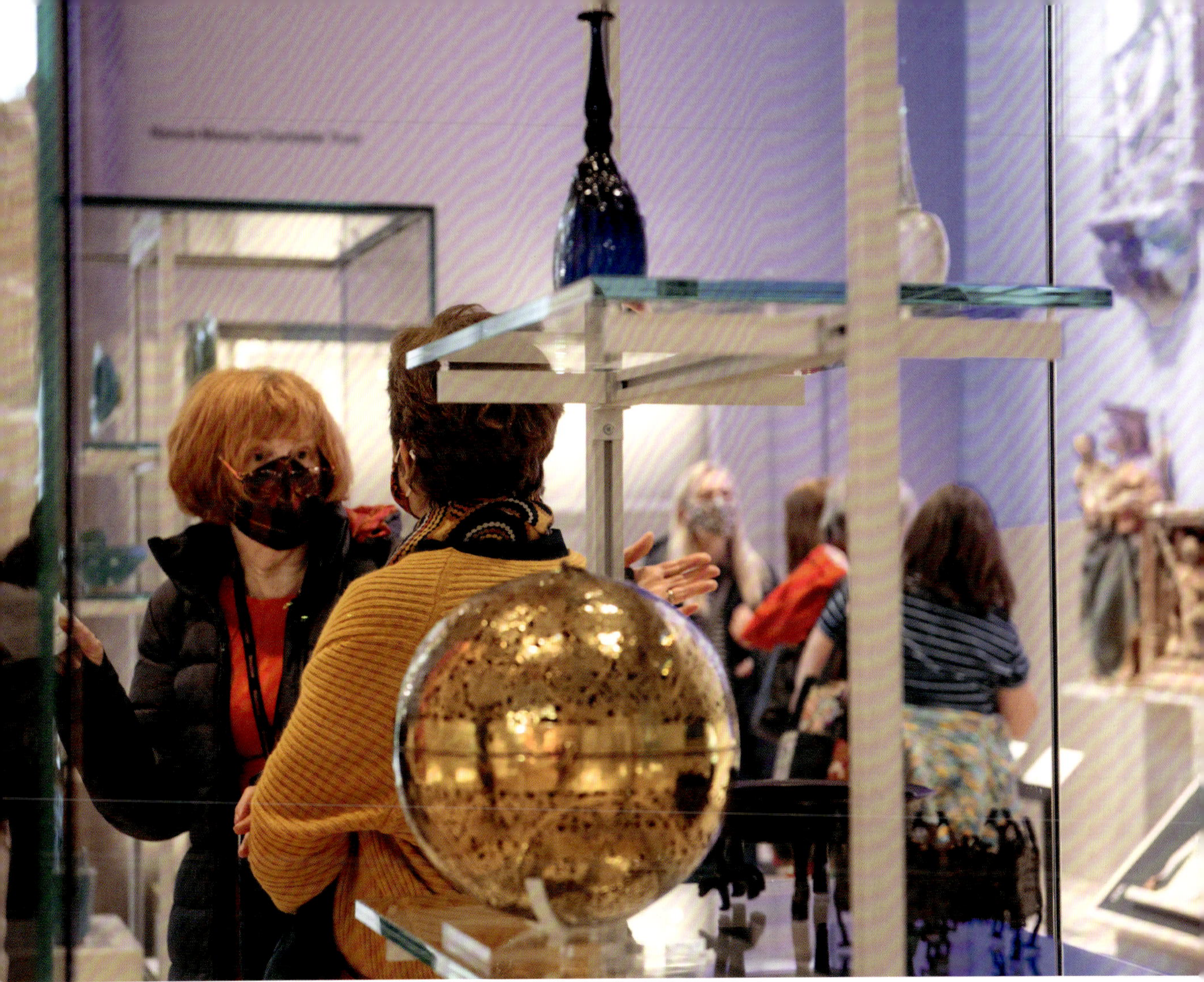

Visitors wearing masks for
protection against Covid-19
at the soft reopening of
the Burrell Collection in
March 2022.

ENVIRONMENTAL SUSTAINABILITY

A principal objective of the refurbishment was to create an economically and environmentally sustainable museum. This was achieved by greatly improving the building envelope fabric to increase thermal performance and airtightness, aiming to reduce energy demands on services and plant and to promote an overall improvement in energy efficiency – a 'fabric first' passive-design approach. Arup was appointed to provide specialist building envelope performance expertise within the design team and to ensure the benefits of this approach were fully realised.

The 'fabric first' approach provided a stable internal environment that allowed Atelier Ten, the services consultant, to design a lean but intelligent services and plant infrastructure. Detailed energy calculations and simulated modelling, including occupancy profiling and collection object conservation assessments, were undertaken, and heat-energy recovery strategies were implemented to ensure minimal energy waste within the building.

The building envelope works were substantial, involving the full replacement of the roofing system and approximately 90 per cent of external façade elements – only the original pink Locharbriggs stone walls and the original cladding glazing frames and supports were retained. All of the existing glazing units were replaced with new high-specification glass to provide better environmental conditions and light control for both the occupants and the collection. Despite the scale of the intervention, this was a heritage-sensitive approach. To maintain the historical integrity of the façade, the replacement elements accurately replicated the original design and aesthetic down to the very smallest details, including the hue of the original glass, leaving no visible trace of this significant intervention in the completed project.

The large expanses of glazing on the façade and roof are unusual for a museum building, but were an important aspect of Gasson's structuralist ideology and aesthetic. To determine the most appropriate glass performance characteristics for the building, detailed calculations and analysis of solar heat gains, natural and artificial light were carried out, looking at sun paths throughout the year, orientation, occupant comfort and the needs of specific objects on display. Optimising the glass not only contributed to reduced energy demand; it also provided information that determined the optimal placement of objects for visitor appreciation and for their conservation, highlighting the link between sustainability and conservation even at the curatorial level.

Arup also piloted a study to benchmark the benefits of recycling glass and ensuring that none of the 3,120m^2 of glass went to landfill.[21] Adopting the principles

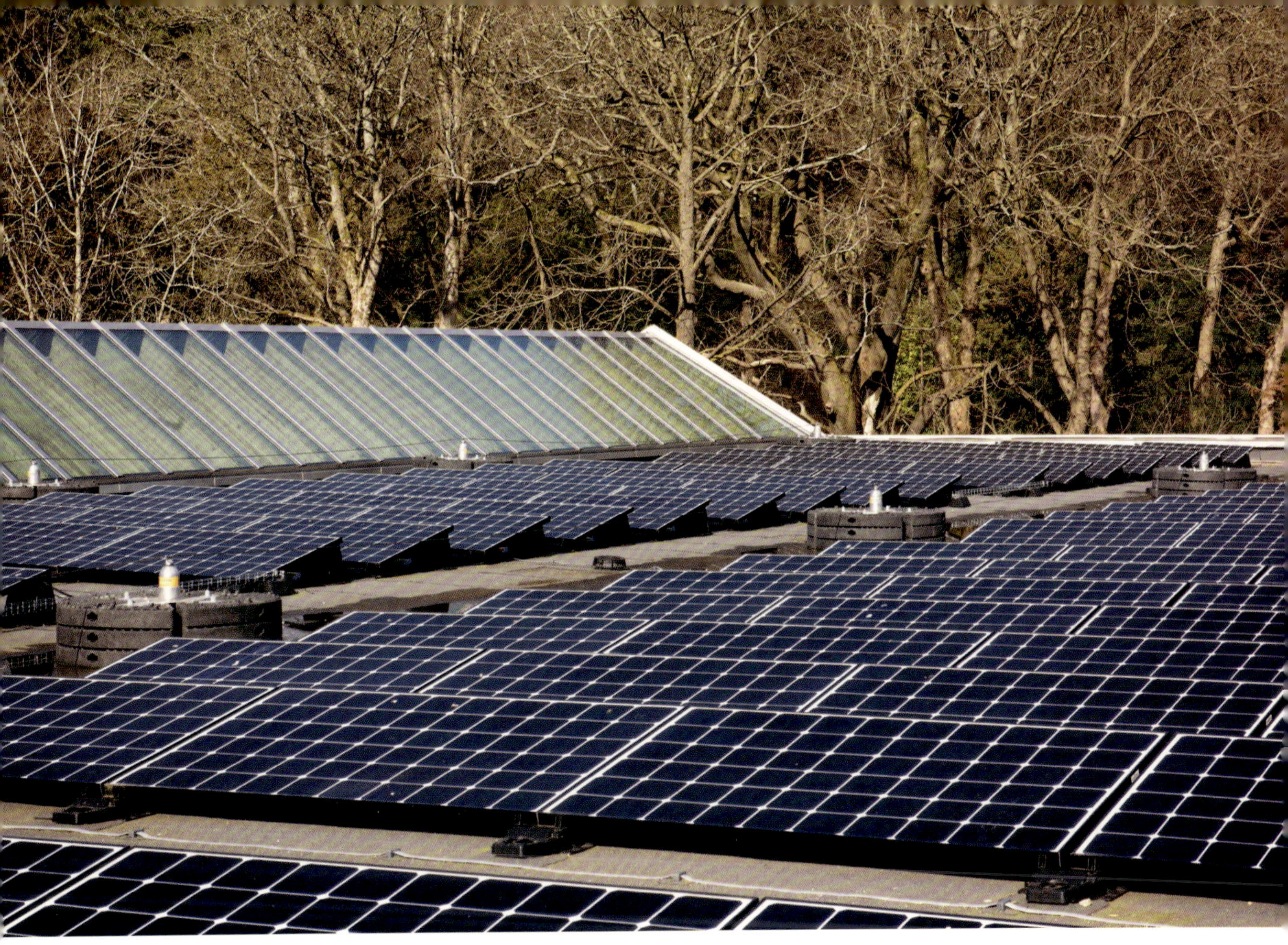

The solar farm on the roof of the Burrell Collection.

of a circular economy, all of the original glass removed from the museum was recycled, resulting in 80 tonnes of it being repurposed for other construction products, with 16 tonnes recycled into architectural glass.

To maintain the integrity of the architectural heritage the original cladding frames were retained and retrofitted with a bespoke design gasket to minimise thermal bridging. Retaining these frames provided a saving of 100 tonnes of embodied CO_{2e} and an annual operational saving of 36 tonnes of CO_{2e} per year – a win-win outcome. The upgraded thermal performance of the roof provided an annual CO_{2e} saving of 220 tonnes per year, and the new photovoltaic solar panels provide a further saving of 200 tonnes per year.

With regards to harnessing energy-generation potential, this was again factored in from the outset and achieved without impacting the original aesthetic. The 384 photovoltaic panels installed on the flat roof, which are not visible from ground level, have created a solar-active area of approximately 665 square metres, which equates to a total potential peak power output of 140 kilowatts, or an average electrical consumption of 150 two-bedroom apartments.[22]

To preserve the architectural heritage, the original services distribution ductwork had to be retained, but when air-pressure tested was found to have around 60 per cent leakage. Atelier Ten's solution was to blow an aerosolised sealant through the ducts which allowed the sealant particles to attach to the inner walls of the ductwork and seal the leakage gaps in the system. The resultant air-pressure test results showed that leakage had been reduced to below 5 per cent.[23]

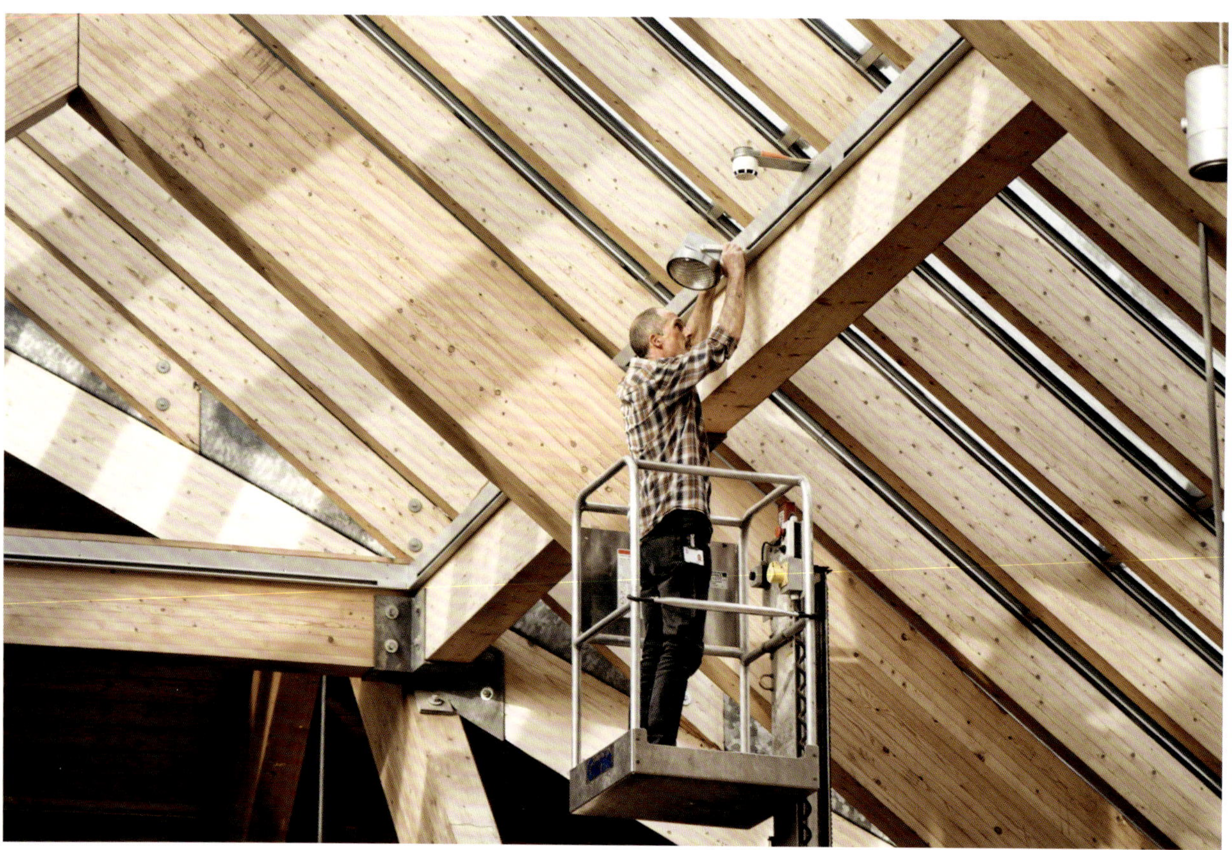

Light fittings were removed before construction and retained for reuse.

Atelier Ten remained on the project post-opening to work with Glasgow Life Museums' Facilities Management Team and the museum staff on a post-occupancy evaluation of energy usage and environmental conditions over an initial three-year period, which was a key element of the energy-conservation strategy from the outset. To ensure the evaluation was effective, the building management system includes an extensive network of environmental monitoring sensors that gather a significant amount of data. Integrated Environmental Solutions, a world-leading Glasgow-based building performance company, was also employed to provide specialist software and expertise in building energy and carbon management computation modelling.

The team collaborated in the evaluation of this information alongside real-life understanding of occupancy profiles and behaviours, which resulted in adaptations to the building services operating model. In the first full year this achieved a 50 per cent reduction in energy usage from the original building benchmark, which is impressive considering the large amount of additional modern services and digital content within the museum. The real value test of improvements to economical sustainability are the energy costs savings. The figures for the first full year of evaluation reported a financial energy saving of £530,000, with an additional projected estimate saving over the next five years of £2.19 million.

Throughout the project, all decisions were tested against sound sustainability criteria. Careful consideration of aspects such as material selection and the utilisation of sustainable local supply chains were central to the process, and developing and retaining local conservation skills and knowledge were also key features of the project.

To measure overall positive environmental impacts, the British Research Establishments Environmental Assessment Method (BREEAM) was adopted, and used primarily as a management tool to keep the project and client team focused on sustainability matters. A BREEAM rating of 'Excellent' was achieved, placing the project in the top 10 per cent in the UK, a significant attainment for a Category A-listed heritage refurbishment.

Recognising the wider environmental impacts of the building's location, the project team developed an active travel plan that encourages sustainable and free travel to the museum. This also encourages visitors to explore the Burrell Collection's natural setting – Pollok Country Park. Notable interventions are a free electric bus (at the time of writing), and new pedestrian and cycle routes that connect museum visitors to the park's other attractions, and which are now also connected to the city's wider cycle network.

WELCOMING BACK VISITORS

King Charles III formally opened the refurbished building on 13 October 2022, marking a seminal moment in the Burrell Collection's story – his mother Queen Elizabeth II had opened the original Burrell on 21 October 1983, almost 40 years previously.

Within its first year of opening, recorded visitor numbers increased to over half a million, and revealed that 45 per cent of visitors were from Glasgow, a further 45 per cent came from outside Scotland, and the remaining 10 per cent from the rest of Scotland. Notably, 74 per cent had visited Pollok Country Park for the first time.

Public reception has been incredibly favourable and central to positive visitor experience is the building itself, its location within Pollok Country Park, and the many different methods of interpretation that allow people to connect with the collection.

Access and environmental sustainability improvements now meet modern standards, and the new displays and curatorial interpretation tell richer and more engaging stories for a contemporary audience. But one of the most significant achievements of the museum is its connection with the local communities. According to a teacher at the local St Conval's Primary School:

For us, one of the real strengths of the museum partnership is the connections the children have made to the artefacts and the Burrell itself. The incredible collection gives the children's learning context and allows them to make real-life connections to the past.[24]

This level of engagement with local communities will ensure the museum has a sustainable future and will continue to enrich the lives of future generations of visitors.

The 'new' Burrell Collection also received much academic and industry acclaim, winning the prestigious Art Fund Museum of the Year in 2023, as it had done in 1985.

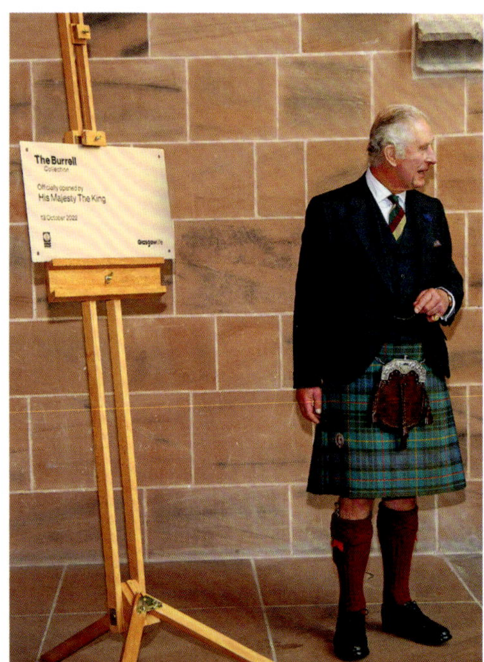

King Charles opening the refurbished Burrell Collection, 13 October 2022.

Children enjoying a visit to the rejuvenated Burrell Collection.

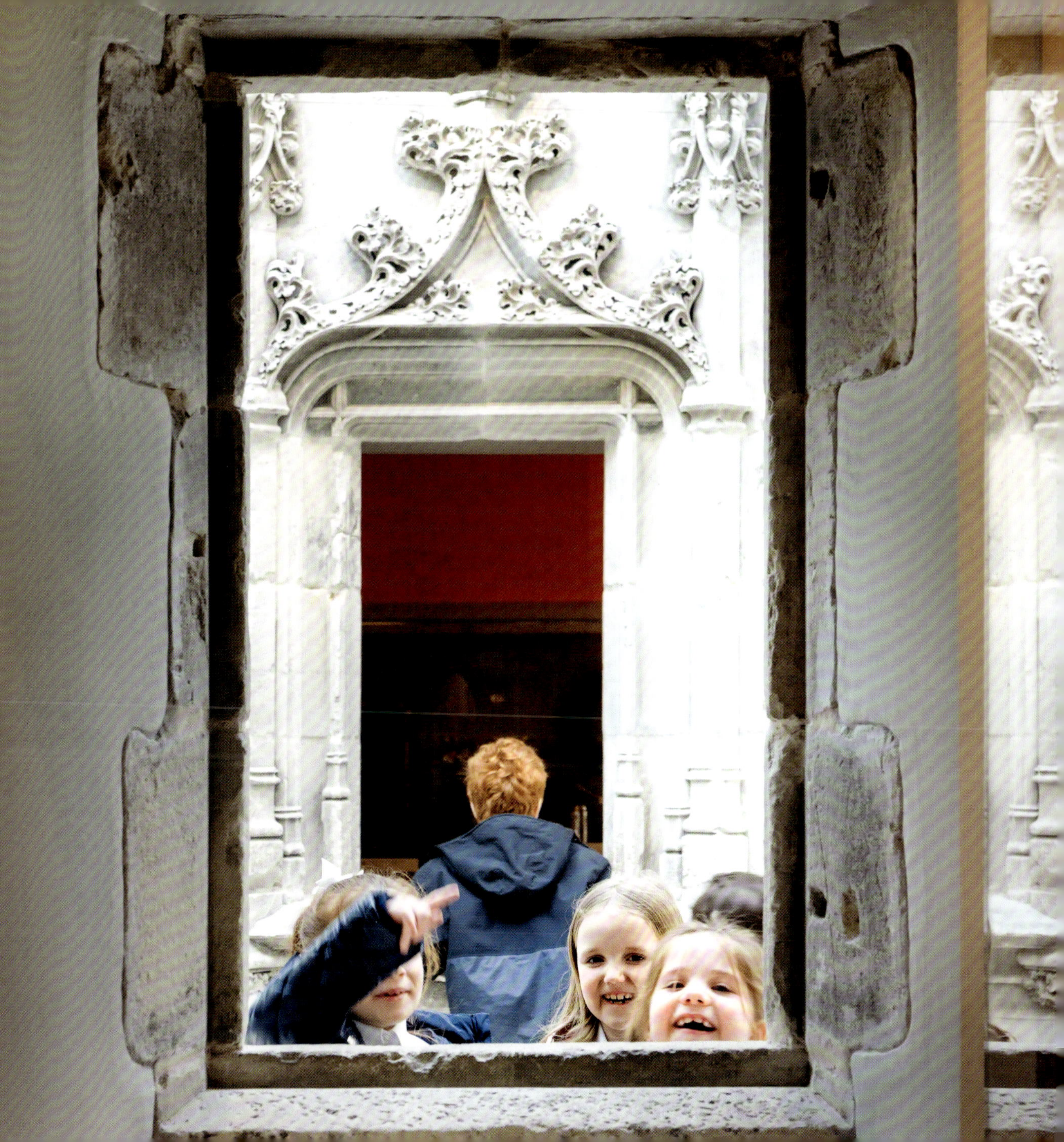

A NEW CULTURAL RENAISSANCE FOR GLASGOW

The Burrell revival already shows signs of sitting at the vanguard of a new and wider renaissance taking place within Glasgow, one that is both culture led as well as climate conscious. As for cities everywhere, responding to global environmental and energy challenges has become imperative, and doing so whilst continuing to care for the rich and complex heritage of Glasgow's past and its people is very much part of the lively, beating heart for which the 'dear green place' is known.

The timber and glass roof structure above Gasson's Italian-style courtyard provides an abundance of natural light from above.

Nursery children were the first to enter the Burrell Collection on reopening day.

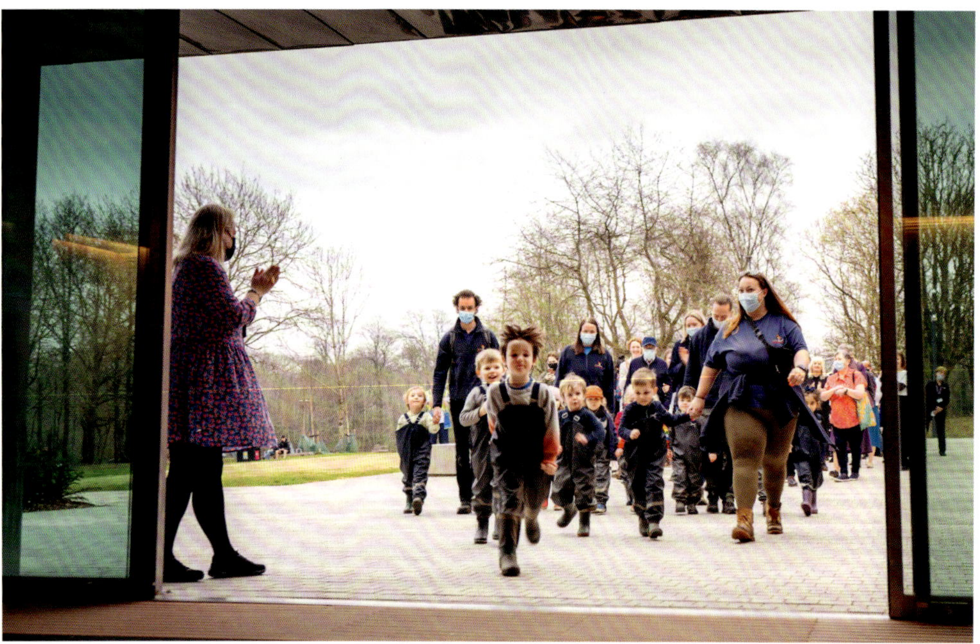

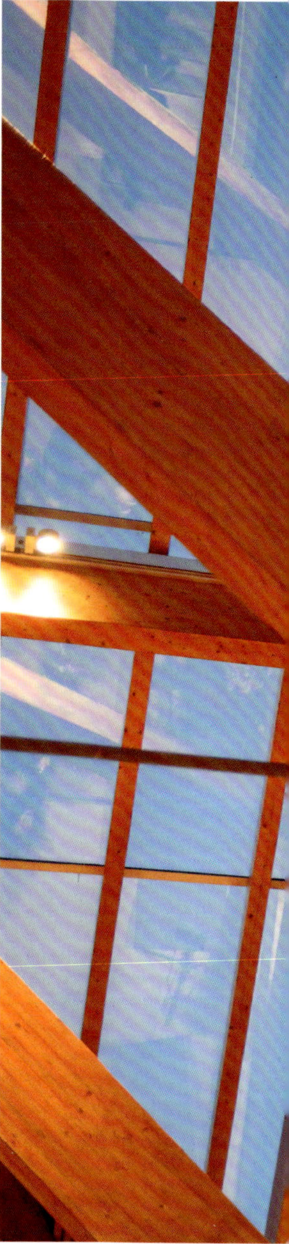

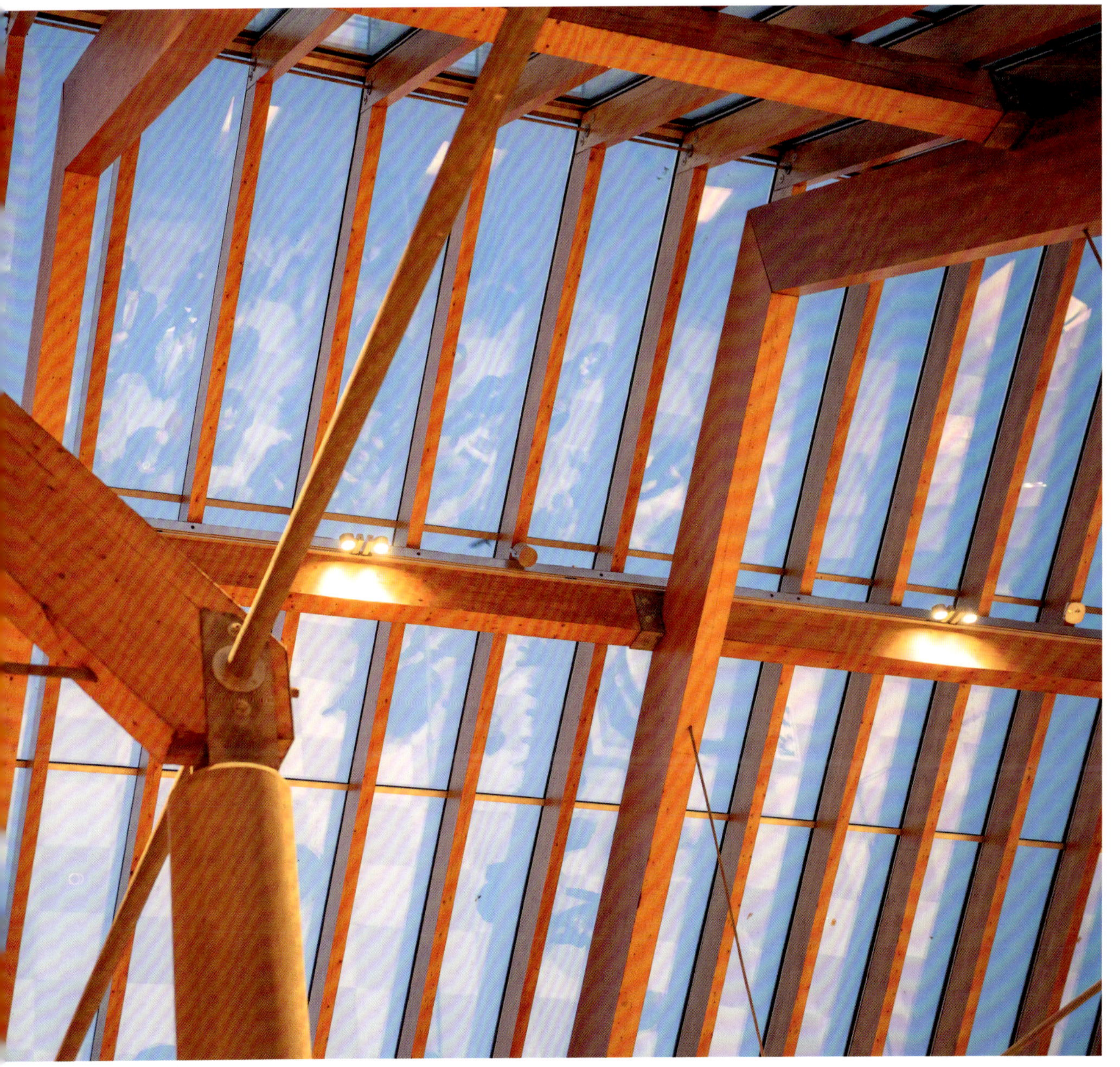

LIST OF AWARDS

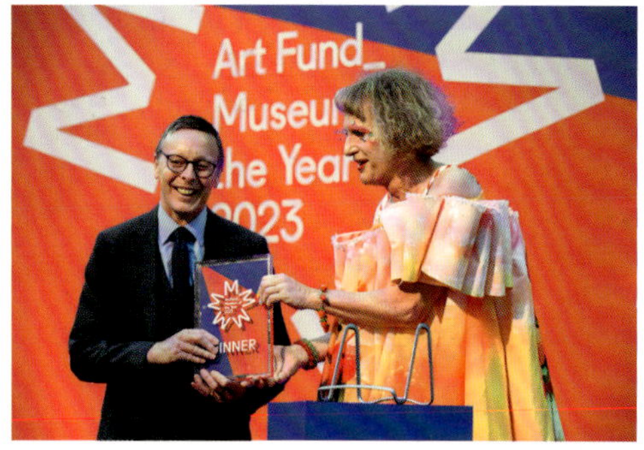

Art Fund Museum of the Year 2023

What the Art Fund judges said:
'They have realised, with real rigour and imagination, the true depth of what it means for a museum to be accessible. I would encourage everyone to go and experience it.'

Royal Incorporation of Architects in Scotland (RIAS) Awards

RIAS Andrew Doolan Best Building in Scotland Award 2024

What the RIAS judges said:
The RIAS jury praised the design for its 'respectful approach' that retains the museum's 'architectural integrity'.

'There was a level of ambition to this project, which was both on the part of the client and obviously the architect, that reflected the importance of the existing building.'

RIAS, Architectural Heritage, Special Category 2024

What the RIAS Special Category Award judges said:
'The judges praised The Burrell Collection as a project where careful consideration was given to every aspect of the design, in order to work with the existing building's architectural language and materials palette.'

Scottish Design Awards 2023

Winner, Design Grand Prix Award

Winner, Architecture: Public Building

Winner, Design for Good Award

Winner, Experiential – Incorporating: audiovisual, graphic and object-based displays

Winner, Moving Imagery Design

What the Scottish Design Awards judges said:
'A big institution reimagining itself doesn't come around often, it prompted me to go back for the first time in 20 years. The well-written entry shows that they care.'

Sir Grayson Perry presents Duncan Dornan, then Head of Glasgow Life Museums and Collections, with the Art Fund Museum of the Year award 2023. Photographer Hydar Dewachi.

British Construction Industry Awards 2022

Winner, Project of the Year

Winner, Cultural and Leisure Category

What the British Construction Industry judges said:
'Working with a listed building, the team went to great lengths to preserve and enhance the existing building, reusing fabric where they could.'

'An exemplar for the future of the industry, positively contributing to both the local community and our planet.'

Architects' Journal Awards

AJ Architecture Awards, Cultural Award 2022

AJ Architecture Awards, Heritage Award 2022

AJ Retrofit Awards, Cultural and Religious Building 2023

What the AJ judges said:
'Truly exemplary…A sophisticated, sensitive, seamless refurbishment.'

Chartered Institution of Building Services Engineers (CIBSE) Façade Design and Engineering Awards 2022

Winner, Refurbishment Project of the Year 2022

Civic Trust Awards

Civic Trust Award, Michael Middleton Special Award 2023

What the Civic Trust judges said:
'The redevelopment of this iconic museum is impressive on every level – welcoming, sustainable, uplifting and calm.'

Association of Cultural Enterprise Awards 2023

Best Shop

Endnotes

1 Sir Hector Hetherington, Principal of the University of Glasgow, at the opening of an exhibition of highlights from the Burrell Collection at Kelvingrove Art Gallery and Museum, Glasgow, 1946. See 'Glasgow art treasures: Burrell Collection on view', *The Scotsman*, 18 May 1946, p. 2.

2 Martin Bellamy and Isobel MacDonald, *William Burrell: A Collector's Life* (Edinburgh, 2022), p. xvi.

3 Scotland (Burrell Art Collection), *Hansard*, Volume 728, debated on Wednesday 11 May 1966: https://hansard.parliament.uk/commons/1966-05-11/debates/bfb923a8-973b-4065-8779-c5e51b46b419/Scotland(BurrellArtCollection).

4 Alfred Russel Wallace, 'Museums for the people', *Macmillan's Magazine*, vol. 19, 1869, pp. 244–50.

5 See www.glasgowlife.org.uk/libraries/family-history/stories-and-blogs-from-the-mitchell/times-past-blogs/bruce-report-times-past.

6 Sir William Burrell to Dr Tom Honeyman, 3 September 1947, Glasgow Museums Archive, GMA.2013.1.2.22.

7 Ibid.

8 Joanna Eley, 'Urban design competitions: A British perspective', *Journal of Architectural and Planning Research*, vol. 7, no. 2, 1990, pp. 132–41.

9 Barnabas Calder, 'Castles, Cows and Glasshouses: the Burrell Collection architectural competition', *Twentieth Century Architecture*, no. 10, 2012, pp. 36–49.

10 Architectural Competition Stage 1 General Information B.3.2.4. Burrell Collection Archives, GMA.2013.1.7.2.1.

11 Alex Gordon and Peter Cannon-Brookes, 'Housing the Burrell collection: a forty-year saga', *International Journal of Museum Management and Curatorship*, vol. 3, no. 1, 1984, pp. 19–59.

12 Ibid., p. 41.

13 Barry Gasson and John Meunier, Basic Principles, Second Report, The Burrell Collection, 1 April 1973, Burrell Collection Archives, GMA.2013.1.7.2.3.

14 *New York Times*, 6 November 1983; *Globe and Mail*, 5 November 1983; *Wall Street Journal*, 14 September 1984.

15 'Barry's Burrell Gallery: special report', *Architects' Journal*, 19 October 1983, pp. 57–103.

16 Richard Demarco, 'The Burrell: a case for art', in ibid., p. 59.

17 *Burrell Voices*, Glasgow Museums Publishing, 2022.

18 Elizabeth Cleland and Lorraine Karafel, *Glasgow Museums: Tapestries from the Burrell Collection* (London, 2017).

19 Event Communications Ltd (Esther Dugdale and Abby Coombs), The Burrell Collection, Renaissance Project, Visitor Experience Concept Design, November 2016, p. 9.

20 Ibid., p. 40.

21 Russell Cole and Graeme DeBrincat, with technical input from David Cameron, 'Vision of the future: Using circular economy principles to sensitively refurbish a heritage listed building, *The Arup Journal*, issue 1, 2023, pp. 15–19.

22 David Cameron, 'Glasgow's Burrell Collection reaching new sustainability standards', The Burrell Collection Blog, 10 November 2021: https://burrellcollection.com/the-burrell-blog-insights-from-the-project-team/glasgow-s-burrell-collection-reaching-new-sustainability-standards/.

23 Andy Pearson, 'Burrell Collection retrofit: a glazing success', *CIBSE Journal*, September 2022: www.cibsejournal.com/case-studies/burrell-collection-retrofit-a-glazing-success/.

24 'The Burrell Collection, Glasgow marks first anniversary of reopening after major refurbishment', The Burrell Collection, 29 March 2023: https://burrellcollection.com/news/the-burrell-collection-glasgow-marks-first-anniversary-of-reopening-after-major-refurbishment/.

Image credits

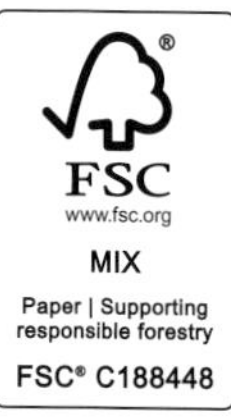